GEOLOGY
OF THE
GREAT
PLAINS
AND MOUNTAIN WEST

INVESTIGATE HOW THE EARTH WAS FORMED

with **15** PROJECTS

CYNTHIA LIGHT BROWN
Illustrated by Eric Baker

~Titles in the *Build It Yourself* Series~

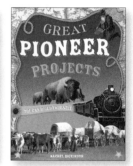

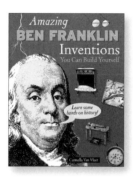
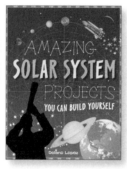

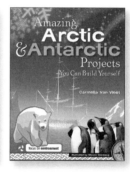

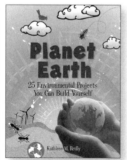

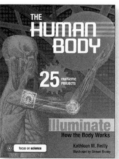

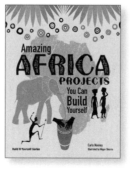

FOOD
25 AMAZING PROJECTS
INVESTIGATE THE HISTORY AND SCIENCE OF WHAT WE EAT

Kathleen M. Reilly

GEORGE WASHINGTON
25 GREAT PROJECTS
YOU CAN BUILD YOURSELF

Build it Yourself Series

Carla Mooney

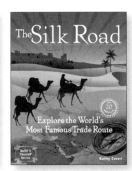

The Silk Road
Explore the World's Most Famous Trade Route

Build It Yourself Series

Kathy Ceceri

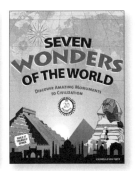

SEVEN WONDERS OF THE WORLD
DISCOVER AMAZING MONUMENTS TO CIVILIZATION

Carmella Van Vleet

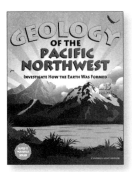

GEOLOGY OF THE PACIFIC NORTHWEST
INVESTIGATE HOW THE EARTH WAS FORMED

CYNTHIA LIGHT BROWN

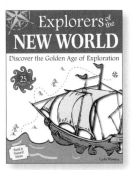

Explorers of the NEW WORLD
Discover the Golden Age of Exploration

Build it Yourself Series

Carla Mooney

Garbage
Investigate What Happens When You Throw It Out

Build it Yourself

DONNA LATHAM

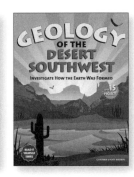

GEOLOGY OF THE DESERT SOUTHWEST
INVESTIGATE HOW THE EARTH WAS FORMED

CYNTHIA LIGHT BROWN

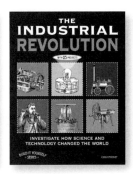

THE INDUSTRIAL REVOLUTION
WITH 25 PROJECTS

INVESTIGATE HOW SCIENCE AND TECHNOLOGY CHANGED THE WORLD

BUILD IT YOURSELF SERIES

CARLA MOONEY

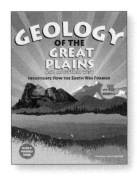

GEOLOGY OF THE GREAT PLAINS AND MOUNTAIN WEST
INVESTIGATE HOW THE EARTH WAS FORMED

CYNTHIA LIGHT BROWN

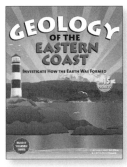

GEOLOGY OF THE EASTERN COAST
INVESTIGATE HOW THE EARTH WAS FORMED

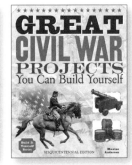

GREAT CIVIL WAR PROJECTS
You Can Build Yourself

SESQUICENTENNIAL EDITION

Maxine Anderson

PROYECTOS IMPRESIONANTES DE LA GUERRA CIVIL
Que Puedes Construir Tú Mismo

EDICIÓN ESPECIAL 150 ANIVERSARIO

Maxine Anderson

MAYA
Amazing Inventions You Can Build Yourself

Build It Yourself Series

MAYA
Inventos Increíbles Que Puedes Construir Tú Mismo

Serie "Construyendo Tú Mismo"

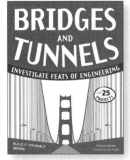

BRIDGES AND TUNNELS
INVESTIGATE FEATS OF ENGINEERING

WITH 25 PROJECTS

BUILD IT YOURSELF SERIES

Donna Latham

Robotics
DISCOVER THE SCIENCE AND TECHNOLOGY OF THE FUTURE

WITH 20 PROJECTS

BUILD IT YOURSELF SERIES

Kathy Ceceri

green press
INITIATIVE

Nomad Press is committed to preserving ancient forests and natural resources. We elected to print *Geology of the Great Plains and Mountain West: Investigate How the Earth Was Formed* on 4,507 lbs. of Williamsburg Recycled 30 percent offset.

Nomad Press made this paper choice because our printer, Sheridan Books, is a member of Green Press Initiative, a nonprofit program dedicated to supporting authors, publishers, and suppliers in their efforts to reduce their use of fiber obtained from endangered forests. For more information, visit **www.greenpressinitiative.org**

This book was manufactured by Sheridan Books,
Ann Arbor, MI USA.
December 2011, Job # 331943
ISBN: 978-1-936313-86-0

Illustrations by Eric Baker
Educational Consultant Marla Conn

Questions regarding the ordering of this book should be addressed to
Independent Publishers Group
814 N. Franklin St.
Chicago, IL 60610
www.ipgbook.com

Nomad Press
2456 Christian St.
White River Junction, VT 05001
www.nomadpress.net

CONTENTS

GEOLOGY & GEOGRAPHY

The Great Plains and Mountain West form the heartland of the United States. This area in the middle of the country has land rippling with wheat and corn. It has towering, majestic mountains. And it has the most destructive tornadoes in the world.

The Great Plains and Mountain West also contain some of our nation's greatest natural wonders. Maybe you live near the mighty Mississippi River. Maybe you have visited the Great Lakes, or explored Yellowstone National Park.

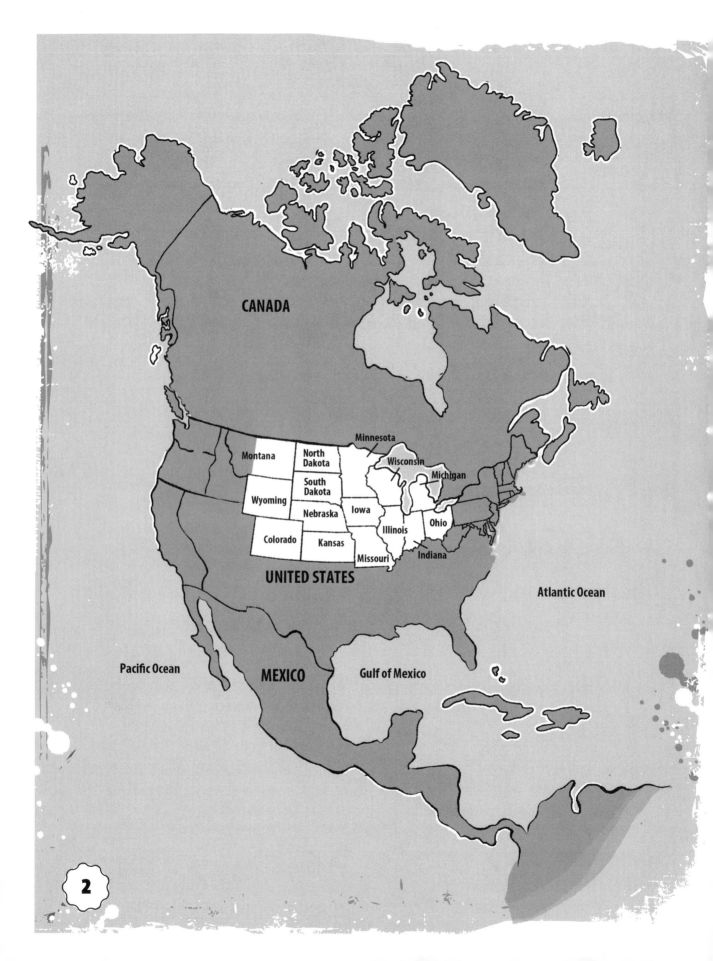

CANADA

Montana

North
Dakota

Minnesota

Wisconsin

South
Dakota

Michigan

Wyoming

Nebraska

Iowa

Illinois

Ohio

Colorado

Kansas

Missouri

Indiana

UNITED STATES

Atlantic Ocean

Pacific Ocean

MEXICO

Gulf of Mexico

Why do the **plains** of **the Midwest** spread out flat like a pancake? How did the Rocky Mountains, which rise so high, form right next to these plains? Even though the central part of the North American continent doesn't have exploding volcanoes, lots of changes have happened there over billions and billions of years.

In this book, you'll learn about the **geology** and physical **geography** of the Great Plains and Mountain West. You'll read about the forces that have shaped the region's mountains, plains, rivers, weather, and **ecosystems**. And you'll discover some interesting facts about the area.

Did you know that earthquakes in Missouri have caused waves in the Mississippi River to travel upstream? Or that the Great Lakes hold one fifth of the **freshwater** of the entire world? As you read through this book, you'll get to work on a lot of exciting experiments and projects. They will help you understand new concepts, like how a flood happens.

WORDS TO KNOW

plains: a flat expanse of land.

the Midwest: another name for the Great Plains in the middle of the United States.

geology: the scientific study of the history and physical nature of the earth.

geography: the study of the earth and its features, especially the shape of the land, and the effect of human activity.

ecosystem: a community of plants and animals living in the same area and relying on each other to survive.

freshwater: water that is not salty.

GEOLOGY: MORE THAN JUST ROCKS

Most people think of geology as the study of rocks. Geology certainly includes that, but it's much more. When you look at a rock, you can describe its color and shape. But what is even more interesting is how that rock formed and how it got to its present location. That involves seeing the big picture—the picture of the whole earth.

Geology is the scientific study of the history and physical nature of the earth. It explains how the color and shape of a rock gives clues to the history of that rock.

Geology involves the huge movements of the earth's **crust**. It also involves the systems of the **atmosphere** and **hydrosphere**, because air and water affect the breakdown and formation of rocks. And the geology of the Great Plains and Mountain West is part of the geologic story of our nation and the earth.

GEOGRAPHY: MORE THAN JUST STATES AND CAPITALS

Just as geology is about more than just rocks, geography is about more than just states and their capitals. These are important, but geography tells a bigger story.

There are two parts to geography. Physical geography includes things like mountains, rivers, **climate**, and the shape of the land. The second part of geography, called cultural geography, is how people interact with the land. An example of cultural geography would be how farming changes the soil of a region. Cultural geography includes things like population, agriculture, and recreation. If you live in the Rocky Mountains you might spend your winters skiing because there are steep slopes with plenty of snow.

WORDS TO KNOW

crust: the thick, outer layer of the earth.

atmosphere: the air surrounding the earth.

hydrosphere: the earth's water, including oceans, rivers, lakes, glaciers, and water vapor in the air.

climate: the average weather of an area over a long period of time.

This book covers the states of Montana, Wyoming, Colorado, North Dakota, South Dakota, Nebraska, Kansas, Minnesota, Iowa, Missouri, Wisconsin, Illinois, Michigan, Indiana, and Ohio.

Look at the map and you'll see that this is a huge area right in the middle of the United States. Are you ready to take a ride on a riverboat down the Mississippi River, whirl around inside a tornado, and climb down into a silver mine! Let's go!

CHAPTER 1

PLATE TECTONICS
SHAPE OUR LAND AND SEA

The Great Plains stretch out flat for hundreds of miles. Then the Plains rise sharply into the rugged, high Rocky Mountains. How did these regions form and why do they look so different from each other?

To understand the driving force behind the formation of the different landscapes in the Great Plains and Mountain West, you first need to understand **plate tectonics**.

WORDS TO KNOW

plate tectonics: the theory that describes how plates move across the earth and interact with each other to produce earthquakes, volcanoes, and mountains.

WORDS TO KNOW

volcano: a vent in the earth's surface through which magma, ash, and gases erupt.

earthquake: a sudden movement in the outer layer of the earth. It releases stress built up from the motion of the earth's plates.

erosion: the wearing away and carrying off of materials on the earth's surface.

brittle: describes a solid that breaks when put under pressure. A blade of grass will bend, but a dry twig is brittle and will break.

mantle: the middle layer of the earth. The upper mantle, together with the crust, forms the lithosphere.

dense: tightly packed.

lithosphere: the rigid outer layer of the earth that includes the crust and the upper mantle.

Plate tectonics is the theory that the outer layer of the earth is made up of interconnected plates that move around. Together with the heat from the sun, the powerful forces inside the earth shape every landscape and ecosystem on the surface of the earth. **Volcanoes**, mountains, valleys, plains, **earthquakes**, and **erosion** all happen when and where they do because of the movement of the earth's plates. To understand plate tectonics, first let's look inside the earth.

A PEEK INSIDE

The earth may look solid and motionless, but much of it is liquid. It consists of three layers.

The crust is the thin, outer layer of the earth. This is the layer that we walk on. It's solid but **brittle**, which means that it breaks when under pressure.

The **mantle** is the layer below the crust. It is hotter and **denser** here because the temperature and pressure inside the earth increase the deeper you go. The upper mantle is brittle and solid. Together, the crust and the upper mantle form the **lithosphere**, or the hard outer layer of the earth.

The lithosphere is broken into plates. Below the plates is a layer of the mantle called the **asthenosphere**. It is partially **molten** and can flow slowly without breaking—a bit like Silly Putty.

The **core** is the center of the earth. It is extremely dense and made up of iron and nickel. There's an inner core, which is solid because the pressure is so great, and an outer core, which is liquid.

The core is almost as hot as the sun—about 9,000 degrees Fahrenheit (5,000 degrees Celsius)!

Did You Know?

You might have heard of the earth's plates being sections of the earth's crust. That's partly correct. The tectonic plates are made of the crust and the upper mantle, which together are called the lithosphere. But most people just call it the crust because it's easier to remember.

WORDS TO KNOW

asthenosphere: the semi-molten middle layer of the earth that includes the lower mantle. Much of the asthenosphere flows slowly, like Silly Putty.

molten: melted by heat to form a liquid.

core: the center of the earth, composed of the metals iron and nickel. The core has two parts—a solid inner core, and a liquid outer core.

oceanic: in or from the ocean.

continental: relating to the earth's large land masses.

PLATES: THE EARTH'S PUZZLE

The hard outer layer of the earth, the lithosphere, is broken up into about 12 large sections, called plates. There are also several smaller plates. The plates fit together like a jigsaw puzzle. Most of the plates are part **oceanic** and part **continental**. For example, the North American Plate includes nearly all of North America and the western half of the Atlantic Ocean.

The plates are in constant slow motion! That's because the layer just under the plates—the asthenosphere—is very hot. The heat causes the molten rocks there, called **magma**, to move around in huge rotating **currents** called convection cells. These convection cells move the plates above, which are floating like rafts on the hot goo below. The plates also help themselves to move along. The older part of a plate is colder and denser than the newer part. When it sinks into the mantle it pulls the rest of the plate with it and keeps the cycle going. Plates move somewhere between 1 to 6 inches per year (2 to 15 centimeters).

WORDS TO KNOW

magma: partially melted rock below the surface of the earth.

current: a constantly moving mass of liquid.

divergent boundary: where two plates are moving in opposite directions, sometimes called a rift zone. New crust forms at rift zones from the magma pushing through the crust.

rifting: when the lithosphere splits apart.

ON THE EDGE

Volcanoes and earthquakes don't just happen anywhere. They're arranged in patterns. For example, there are lots of volcanoes around the rim of the Pacific Ocean, but there are none in Kansas. That's because most of the action happens where one plate meets another. This is called a plate boundary. There are three different kinds of plate boundaries.

Divergent plate boundaries are where two plates move apart from each other. They do this because the magma beneath is pushing upward. This causes **rifting**. The hot goo pushes out and solidifies to form new rocks. Nearly all of the earth's new crust forms at divergent boundaries. An example of new crust can be found at Craters of the Moon National Monument in Idaho.

Convergent plate boundaries are where two plates collide. What happens depends on whether the plates are oceanic or continental. When an oceanic plate collides with a continental plate, volcanoes form. Because the oceanic plate is denser than the continental plate, it slides underneath the continental plate. This is called **subduction**.

As the subducted oceanic plate sinks lower, its weight pulls the rest of the plate along as well. The sinking plate encounters a lot of heat and pressure. This causes the plate to release hot gas and steam, which rises and melts the rock above. The melted rock, the magma, also rises to the surface, creating volcanoes. It can also compress the continent, causing the crust to buckle.

The Rocky Mountains formed when oceanic crust subducted beneath the North American Plate and caused the crust to buckle.

If a continental plate collides with another continental plate, they both buckle upwards, forming mountains. That's what is happening now where the Indian Plate and the Eurasian Plate are colliding. The result is the Himalaya Mountains, which include the highest mountain in the world, Mt. Everest.

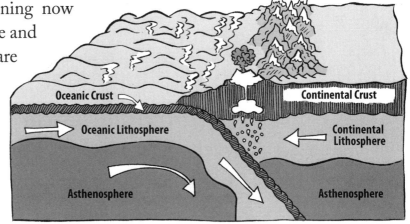

Oceanic-Continental Convergance

WORDS TO KNOW

transform boundary: where two plates slide against each other.

fault: a crack in the outer layer of the earth.

hotspot: an area in the middle of a plate, where hot magma rises to the surface.

tectonic: relating to the forces that produce movement and changes in the earth's crust.

craton: the stable, central part of a continent.

igneous rock: rock that forms from cooling magma.

metamorphic rock: rock that has been transformed by heat or pressure or both into new rock, while staying solid.

Transform plate boundaries are where two plates grind against each other as they move side by side in opposite directions. As the plates move past each other they sometimes suddenly slip. This creates a big lurch, or earthquake.

On the West Coast, the famous San Andreas **Fault** in California is part of a transform boundary between the North American and Pacific Plates. This is why California has so many earthquakes.

Hotspots are other areas of strong geologic activity, but they aren't on the edge of plates. These are volcanic regions that usually occur in the middle of a plate. They exist because extremely hot magma, probably from deep in the mantle, makes its way to the surface. There is a hotspot beneath Yellowstone National Park, where Wyoming, Idaho, and Montana meet.

Did You Know?

The oldest rocks in the United States are found in northern Minnesota in the Minnesota River Valley and northern Michigan. They are between 3.5 and 3.7 billion years old. The oldest rocks on Earth are in northern Canada, and are over 4 billion years old.

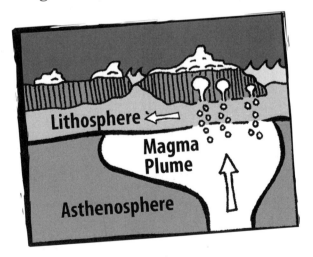

Lithosphere

Magma Plume

Asthenosphere

GIANT CONVEYOR BELT

The movement of the plates acts a bit like a giant, wide conveyor belt. This conveyor belt is like a flat escalator, used to move people or things across a long space. At divergent boundaries, magma pushes the plates apart, cools, and forms new crust.

The lithosphere is like a rigid board, though, and as two plates move apart, the other end of each plate collides with more lithosphere. At the collision point, one plate is subducted, or pushed under, and melts. So lithosphere is created on one end, and destroyed on another. Just like conveyor belts, or the stairs on an escalator, lithosphere appears on one end and disappears on the other end.

TECTONIC HISTORY OF THE GREAT PLAINS AND MOUNTAIN WEST

This area has a long **tectonic** history. Over 2½ billion years ago, small bits of continental and oceanic crust collided and stuck together over time. This process formed the central part of North America, called the **craton**. Mountains were uplifted and volcanoes formed. The rocks in the craton are **igneous** and **metamorphic**. They formed at high pressures and temperatures deep within the crust, at least 10 miles beneath the surface (16 kilometers).

The mountains that formed were probably as high as the Himalaya Mountains of today. This very old part of the craton includes the central section of Canada and the northern Midwest of the United States including parts of Minnesota, Wisconsin, and Michigan.

Craton

**North America
2 Billion Years Ago**

11

The North American continent continued to grow as other pieces of crust were added onto the southern edge of the craton. These newer pieces of crust stretch from what is now Arizona to Missouri.

WORDS TO KNOW

basin: a low area shaped like a bowl.

sediment: loose rock particles such as sand or clay.

sedimentary rock: rock formed from the compression of sediments, the remains of plants and animals, or from the evaporation of seawater.

geologist: a scientist who studies the earth and its movements.

Then, a little over a billion years ago, the continent tried to rift apart. It started in an area in what is now Kansas, extending through Nebraska, Iowa, Minnesota, Wisconsin, and Michigan. The rifting stopped, perhaps because North America began colliding with another continent along its eastern edge. But the rift created a **basin** where Lake Superior is today.

Later, erosion removed layers of rocks in the mountains over many millions of years. Only the "roots" of the ancient mountains remained, leaving land that was a flat rolling plain. When a shallow inland sea covered much of the craton, the seas left sand, mud, and seashells. These **sediments** formed into a thin covering of **sedimentary rocks** over the older rocks.

Craton

Addition

North America 1.8-1.65 Billion Years Ago

Around 80 million years ago, the plates were moving again. Usually, when an oceanic plate collides with a continental plate, volcanoes form close to the boundary.

But this time, as a large oceanic plate was pushing under the North American Plate, the Rocky Mountains formed hundreds of miles inland. Why was there activity so far from the edge of a plate? **Geologists** think that the oceanic plate subducted at a shallow angle. This caused the crust to compress the craton in the middle of the continent, pushing up masses of old, hard rocks to form the Rocky Mountains.

North America 700 Million Years Ago

Exposed Craton

Sediment Blanket

As the Rockies were pushed upward, they were also eroding at the same time.

Sand and mud eroded and was deposited onto the lowlands to the east of the mountains. Ash from volcanoes erupting was carried east by the wind. All of this sediment continued to cover the North American craton.

Finally, in the last 2 million years or so, the northern part of the craton was shaped by **glaciers** that came south during colder periods. These glaciers came as far south as Missouri in the Great Plains region. We are in a warmer period in Earth's history now, and the glaciers have retreated north. They left behind lakes and rivers.

WHAT'S HAPPENING NOW?

The central part of the United States is like the backbone of the country. You can find the oldest rocks here, back to long before other parts of the country existed. The most ancient part is called the North American Craton.

The craton has been undisturbed by tectonic activity for hundreds of millions of years, and it shows. You won't find a lot of active volcanoes here. Even the ancient mountains have been eroded, leaving hundreds of miles of flat earth. Sometimes, though, there can be movement of the crust in areas of ancient rifting, causing earthquakes.

Most of the ancient rocks, or craton, are now covered by a relatively thin layer of younger, sedimentary rocks.

This part of the craton is called the **continental platform**, and includes most of the Great Plains. Areas where the old rocks are exposed on the surface are called the **continental shield**. Most of the continental shield is in Canada, but a section can be found in Michigan, Wisconsin, and Minnesota.

ANCIENT TIME

The rocks in the continental shield are some of the oldest rocks on Earth—over 3 billion years old. How do geologists know how old rocks are? They use different ways to figure out how long ago a rock formed. Some methods work best for shorter time periods, like hundreds or thousands of years. Other methods are better for measuring very long time periods, like millions or billions of years. **Radiometric dating** is used to find the age of the very old igneous and metamorphic rocks in the craton.

When magma cools to form igneous rocks, the rocks contain various **elements**. Some of the elements are radioactive and decay, or break down, over time. This means that the **atoms** lose particles and become a new element. The starting element is called the parent and the stable element it decays into is called the daughter.

Each kind of radioactive element decays at a known rate. For example, scientists know that after 1.25 billion years, one half of the potassium in a rock will have decayed to become argon. This is called the **half-life**. Scientists can measure how much potassium is in a rock sample and compare it to the amount of argon. This helps them to calculate the age of the rock.

WORDS TO KNOW

radiometric dating: a method of determining the age of rocks. It looks at a radioactive element in rock, such as uranium, and measures how much it has decayed.

element: a substance that is made up of atoms that are all the same.

atom: the smallest particle of matter that cannot be broken down without changing the particle's properties. Everything on Earth is made of various combinations of atoms.

half-life: the amount of time it takes for one half of a radioactive parent element to decay to its daughter element.

Did You Know?

Voyageurs National Park in northern Minnesota is a huge region of ancient igneous and metamorphic rocks. The rocks here are over 2.5 billion years old—that's older than the rocks at the bottom of the Grand Canyon. The area has been scoured by glaciers and is now covered by lakes. In fact, you can only get around the park by boat!

PLATE TECTONICS: THE ORIGINAL RECYCLER

The earth has been recycling materials for over 4 billion years! Every rock you see has come from another kind of rock. And every rock you see will eventually become another one. All this recycling is because of the movement of the plates pushing everything around. To understand this recycling, first you have to know a bit about types of rocks.

There are three main types of rocks: igneous, sedimentary, and metamorphic.

Igneous Rocks have formed from the cooling of molten rock. As you go deeper beneath the surface of the earth, it becomes hotter. At around 25 miles beneath the surface (40 kilometers), it's hot enough to melt rocks. When that molten rock, called magma, comes to the surface, it cools into igneous rocks.

Sedimentary Rocks form when small particles of rock, called sediments, are pressed tightly together into rock. Sediments come from other rocks being eroded, or broken into smaller pieces by wind, water, ice, and gravity. Sedimentary rocks can also form from the remains of plants or animals being pressed together. When seawater evaporates, the minerals and salts in the water stay behind and can form into rock.

Metamorphic Rocks form when heat or pressure changes rocks into new rocks. Pressure, like temperature, increases as you go farther beneath the surface of the earth. If rocks are pushed under the surface, but not far enough to melt, they can be changed into new rocks without first melting.

Igneous rocks can be eroded into sediments, which then form sedimentary rocks. Those sedimentary rocks can then be buried and heated and squeezed to form metamorphic rocks. Metamorphic rocks can be pushed down into the mantle and melted, to later form igneous rocks. Or it could happen in reverse, because any type of rock can form from any other type of rock.

MAKE YOUR OWN
WALK THROUGH TIME

It's hard to imagine how old the rocks in the North American Craton are. How much is 2 billion years? Try this activity to put it all in perspective.

Grab a friend who's good at counting. Pick a place where you can walk for 10 minutes without stopping, like a walking path or a school playground. Start walking and count out loud together for every step you take. When you get to the steps listed below, say the step first, then what happened in that "step." Keep walking and counting. Each step you take represents 10 million years!

Step 1	Earth formed (4.6 billion years ago)
Step 57	Oldest rocks on Earth (4.03 billion years ago)
Step 90	Oldest rocks in the United States (3.7 billion years ago)
Step 210	North American continent begins forming (about 2.5 billion years ago)
Step 260	North American craton grows to the south from Arizona to Missouri (1.8 billion years ago)
Step 350	North American craton begins to rift apart (1.1 billion years ago)
Step 390	Inland seas start to flood the interior of North America, depositing sediments (700 million years ago)
Step 406	First abundant life (545 million years ago)
Step 435	First dinosaurs (248 million years ago)
Step 452	Rocky Mountains form (80 million years ago)
Step 455	First dogs (54 million years ago)
Step 459½	First human ancestors (5.5 million years ago)
Step 460	First humans (160,000 years ago)
Step 460	Present day

MAKE YOUR OWN
POPCORN TIME

SUPPLIES

- 6 or more small bags of unpopped microwave popcorn
- marker
- microwave oven
- 5 pieces of paper
- pencil
- graph paper

Go!

1 Using the marker, label 5 popcorn bags with the following: 0 seconds, 10 seconds, 20 seconds, 30 seconds, and 40 seconds. Place one bag of popcorn at a time in the microwave and set the timer for 2 minutes. As soon as the popcorn begins popping, start counting the seconds. After the number of seconds marked on the bag, turn the microwave off and remove the bag. For example, remove the bag labeled 0 seconds as soon as it starts popping.

2 After the bags have cooled down, open each bag and spread the contents on a separate piece of paper. For each bag, count the number of unpopped kernels and the number of popped corn kernels. Record the results, including the number of kernels and popped corn combined.

3 Plot the results on the graph paper. The horizontal axis should be the time, from zero to 50 seconds. The vertical axis should be the percent of the popped kernels. To get the percent of popped kernels for each bag, divide the number of popped corns by the total number of kernels and popped corn.

4 Draw a horizontal line at the 50 percent mark. Also draw a line connecting all of the points you have plotted. Where they cross is the half-life of your popcorn.

5 If you'd like, pop another bag of popcorn for a different time, such as 15 seconds or 25 seconds. Have a friend count the kernels and popped corn, and see if they can guess the amount of time it was popped by using your chart. Did they come close?

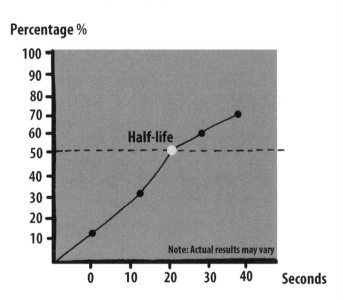

Percentage %

Half-life

Note: Actual results may vary

Seconds

What's Happening?

The kernels are like the parent element in a rock, and the popped corn is like the daughter element. Popcorn has a short half-life compared to elements used to determine the ages of rocks, but the method is similar. Scientists count the number of parent elements compared to the daughter elements to determine the age of the rock. Just like with your popcorn, the more parent elements (kernels) there are, the younger the rock. Do you see a curve to the graph that you made? Radioactivity decreases over time because the fewer parents you have, the slower you lose them. The same is true for the popcorn once it gets going.

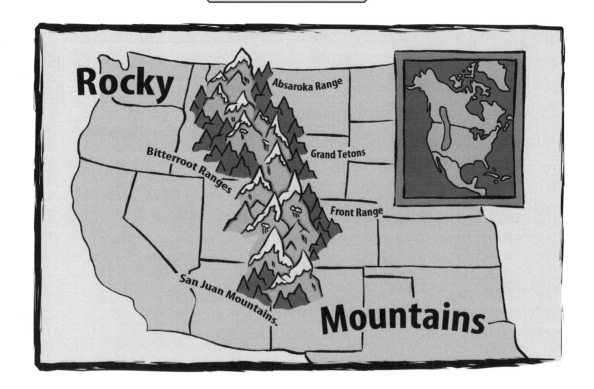

CHAPTER 2

MOUNTAIN RANGES

If you travel west across the relatively flat Great Plains, you come suddenly upon one of the great mountain chains of the world. The Rocky Mountains rise abruptly with spectacular, snow-capped peaks. How did they form? What's there? Let's find out!

ROCKY MOUNTAINS

The Rocky Mountains, often just called the Rockies, are a major mountain chain in North America. The mountains stretch almost 2,000 miles from British Columbia in Canada south to New Mexico (3,200 kilometers). Many smaller mountain ranges make up the Rockies, such as the Grand Tetons in Wyoming and the Front Range in Colorado.

WORDS TO KNOW

Ancestral Rockies: a mountain chain that formed over 300 million years ago. These mountains were eroded, but the rocks formed then can be seen in today's Rocky Mountains.

The rocks that you find in the Rocky Mountains formed long ago, over many millions of years. Some rocks formed from volcanoes, and others during collisions of ancient tectonic plates. These **Ancestral Rockies** eroded over time. Inland seas then flooded most of the interior of North America, which covered these old rocks with sediments.

Then, in the time of the dinosaurs, the North American continent collided with an oceanic plate to the west. When the subduction began, the oceanic plate pushed under North America at a steep angle, which is how subduction normally happens. This formed the Pacific Mountain System in Washington, Oregon, and California.

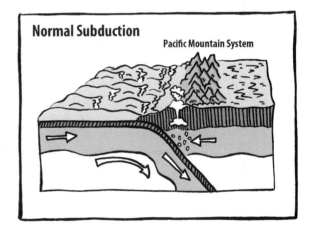

Around 70 to 80 million years ago, geologists think the subduction changed. The oceanic plate started to subduct at a much flatter angle. It caused the rocks far inland to arch into large folds, and piles of rocks were thrust on top of each other. This pushing up of rocks formed the Rocky Mountains. There have been other periods of uplift as well as volcanic activity that have formed smaller ranges in the chain. The Rockies are complicated mountains!

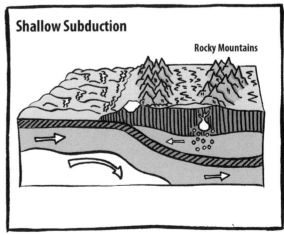

When the Rockies were first uplifted, they were probably much like the Himalayas are today—more than 20,000 feet above sea level (6,096 meters). Scientists estimate that almost 2 miles of sedimentary rocks have eroded away from the top since then (3 kilometers). The older rocks, which are harder, are exposed in most areas.

About 2 million years ago, the earth became cooler and wetter. Glaciers began scraping the mountains. The way the Rockies look today is due to this erosion and the effect of glaciers. Different kinds of rocks erode differently, giving the landscape different shapes. For example, granite is a hard, igneous rock that erodes to rounded forms. Crystalline metamorphic rocks erode to jagged peaks.

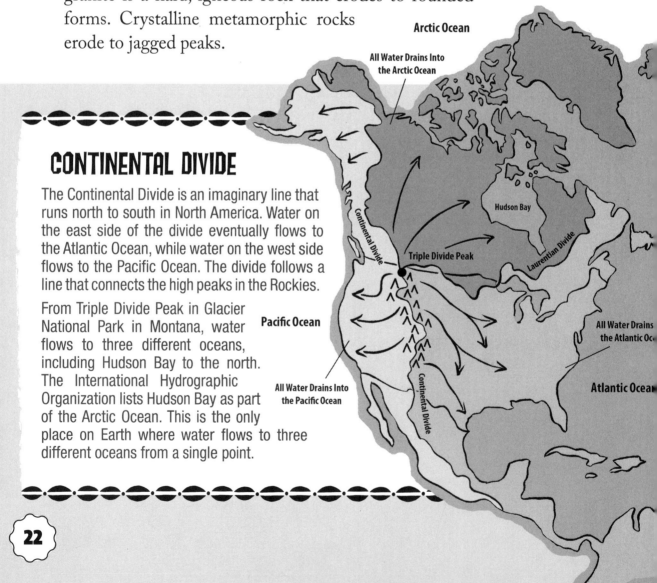

CONTINENTAL DIVIDE

The Continental Divide is an imaginary line that runs north to south in North America. Water on the east side of the divide eventually flows to the Atlantic Ocean, while water on the west side flows to the Pacific Ocean. The divide follows a line that connects the high peaks in the Rockies.

From Triple Divide Peak in Glacier National Park in Montana, water flows to three different oceans, including Hudson Bay to the north. The International Hydrographic Organization lists Hudson Bay as part of the Arctic Ocean. This is the only place on Earth where water flows to three different oceans from a single point.

WILDLIFE

The Rocky Mountains support a variety of plants and animals. They have had to **adapt** to the harsh conditions in many ways.

Mountain goats have hoofs that are rubbery on the underside and sharp around the edges. This helps them grip slippery ledges at the tops of mountains. If you hike in the mountains, the rubbery soles of your hiking boots will stop you from slipping too. Why do mountain goats climb so high? Large **predators** aren't so nimble and won't follow them.

Ptarmigans look a bit like a chicken. While most birds **migrate** to warmer climates in the winter, ptarmigans stay all winter long. When food is scarce, they eat twigs. Ptarmigans have white feathers in the winter, and mottled brown in the summer. This helps them blend into their surroundings and hide from predators. They also grow thick feathers on their feet in the winter to help them walk on top of the snow—just like snowshoes!

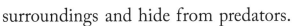

WORDS TO KNOW

adapt: changes a plant or animal makes to survive.

predator: an animal that hunts another animal for food.

migrate: to move from one place to another each year.

Ptarmigan

23

Grizzly bears are found in the northern Rockies. They can grow to 8 feet tall (2½ meters), and weigh as much as three refrigerators (800 pounds/363 kilograms). They love berries and mountain trout, a type of fish found in many mountain streams.

Grizzly Bear

Golden eagles are the largest **birds of prey** in the Rocky Mountains. Females can reach 6½ feet from wing tip to wing tip (2 meters), and can weigh 12 pounds (5½ kilograms).

Golden Eagle

WORDS TO KNOW

bird of prey: a bird that hunts animals for food.

habitat: the natural area where a plant or animal lives.

Bighorn sheep have special hooves to help them jump and climb around cliffs. Thick coats of hair, two layers thick, help them keep warm in frigid conditions. Bighorn sheep are known for their large horns that can weigh up to 30 pounds (14 kilograms). Large male sheep fight by charging at each other and crashing their horns to prove who's the biggest and toughest.

Bighorn Sheep

The number of bighorn sheep declined 100 years ago because of hunting, changes in their **habitat**, and disease. But as people became concerned, the sheep were protected in national parks and by restrictions on hunting. One of the first campaigns to save bighorn sheep was by the Boy Scouts in Arizona. Now there are healthy populations of bighorn sheep throughout the Rockies.

HIGH MOUNTAINS

Pike's Peak is one of the more famous mountains in the Rockies. It is 14,115 feet high (4,302 meters). That's taller than 11 Empire State Buildings stacked on top of each other! It sits right along the edge of the Great Plains, and is visible from far away. Katherine Lee Bates wrote the song "America the Beautiful" in 1893 after seeing the view of the Rockies and the plains from Pike's Peak. Her words, "For purple mountain majesties, Above the fruited plain," refers to the Rockies, which can look purplish from a distance, rising high above the Great Plains. Colorado has 53 mountains that are above 14,000 feet high (4,267 meters).

The highest "mountain" in each state of the region is listed below. You might notice that some states list a "point" or "hill" or "mound" because they don't really have any mountains.

State	Mountain	Height
Colorado	Mt. Elbert	**14,433 feet** (4,399 meters)
Wyoming	Gannett Peak	**13,804 feet** (4,207 meters)
Montana	Granite Peak	**12,799 feet** (3,901 meters)
South Dakota	Harney Peak	**7,242 feet** (2,207 meters)
Nebraska	Panorama Point	**5,424 feet** (1,653 meters)
Kansas	Mt. Sunflower	**4,039 feet** (1,231 meters)
North Dakota	White Butte	**3,506 feet** (1,069 meters)
Minnesota	Eagle Mountain	**2,301 feet** (701 meters)
Michigan	Mt. Arvon	**1,979 feet** (603 meters)
Wisconsin	Timms Hill	**1,951 feet** (595 meters)
Missouri	Taum Sauk Mountain	**1,772 feet** (540 meters)
Iowa	Hawkeye Point	**1,670 feet** (509 meters)
Ohio	Campbell Hill	**1,549 feet** (472 meters)
Indiana	Hoosier Hill Point	**1,257 feet** (383 meters)
Illinois	Charles Mound	**1,235 feet** (376 meters)

alpine glacier: a glacier that forms in the mountains.

cirque: a basin at the head of a glacial valley, which often contains a lake.

U-shaped valley: a valley that has been carved by a glacier and has a shape like the letter "U," with steep sides and a flat floor.

ALPINE GLACIERS

Glaciers are large areas of ice that move. They form when snow falls in the winter and doesn't melt in the summer. The snow gets deeper and heavier and compresses the snow crystals, which lock together. **Alpine glaciers** often form in the highest mountains because it is so cold there, but they are much smaller than the large sheets of ice that cover continents. The Wind River Range has 63 glaciers, the most in the American Rocky Mountains. Glaciers can be found throughout the Rockies.

Alpine glaciers in the Rockies are mostly **cirque** glaciers. Snow can accumulate in these bowl-shaped areas at the head of valleys high in the mountains, forming small, round glaciers. If a cirque glacier later melts, it often forms a lake or pond.

During the past 2 million years, there have been many periods when the earth was much colder. This allowed glaciers to come farther down the mountains into the valleys. For example, the glaciers in Glacier National Park have formed and melted many times. The ones there today formed in the last few thousand years as the climate became colder. They are shrinking today as the climate becomes warmer.

As larger glaciers move, they pick up rocks and even boulders, which carve the landscape. Here are some things to look for that tell you a glacier has been around:

Cirques: These large bowls that form at the top, or head, of a glacier often fill with water, forming a small lake. It looks almost like a giant took a big scoop of ice cream out of the mountain. There are cirques throughout the Rockies.

U-Shaped Valleys: River valleys are V-shaped, from the river slowly cutting into the rock. Glaciers follow the path of rivers because, like rivers, they are seeking the fastest way downhill. But glaciers are wider, and the rocks they carry carve out a valley with a "U" shape.

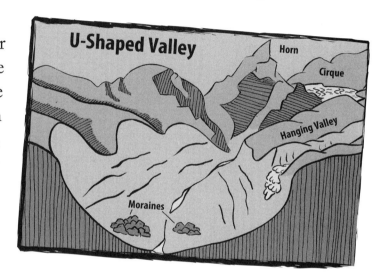

Even though they are slow, glaciers are extremely powerful. They move aside just about anything in their way—trees, rocks, and even large boulders.

Glaciers become a bit like sandpaper as they pluck up rocks and carry them downhill. This sandpaper erodes the land into **U-shaped valleys** and sharp mountain peaks. In Rocky Mountain National Park, there are numerous U-shaped valleys including Forest Canyon and Fall River Valley. McDonald Valley in Glacier National Park is another great example of a U-shaped valley.

Did You Know?

The mountains in the Never Summer Range in the Rocky Mountains of Colorado are snow-capped throughout the year.

Hanging Valleys: When a smaller glacier in a side canyon feeds into a larger glacier, the smaller glacier doesn't cut as deeply as the larger glacier. After they melt, the smaller glaciers leave behind smaller valleys high up on the mountainsides that look like they're hanging. You can drive around the rim of a valley called "Hanging Valley" in Rocky Mountain National Park. In Glacier National Park, a waterfall called Birdwoman Falls spills from a **hanging valley** on Mt. Oberlin.

Polished Rocks: As the glacier drags smaller rocks over bedrock below, the smaller rocks grind a smooth or grooved surface.

Moraines: Remember how glaciers pick up lots of rocks? What happens when the glacier melts at the bottom? The rocks are dumped out. Because the glacier acts like a conveyor belt made out of ice, more and more rocks are dumped out, forming piles of rocks at the bottom and sides of the glacier. Recent **moraines** look just like a pile of rocks. Older moraines are covered by soil and plants.

Horns: These are steep-sided mountain peaks. They are formed by two or more glaciers carving from different directions. Kinnerly Peak in Glacier National Park and numerous mountains in Grand Tetons National Park are examples of horns created by glaciers.

WORDS TO KNOW

hanging valley: a side valley that joins the main valley at a higher level. It forms when a smaller glacier doesn't erode as deeply as the main glacier.

moraine: an accumulation of gravel and sand deposited at the front of a glacier.

Did You Know?

There are four national parks in the American Rocky Mountains: Glacier National Park in Montana, Yellowstone and Grand Teton National Parks in Wyoming, and Rocky Mountain National Park in Colorado. There are five national parks in the Canadian Rockies.

SNOW AND AVALANCHES

The record for the most snowfall in the Rockies was set in the winter of 1978–1979, when 70 feet of snow fell on Wolf Creek Pass in Colorado (21 meters). That's as high as a six-story building! Deep snow causes avalanches, and avalanches are common in the Rockies. They are huge masses of snow, ice, and rocks that slide down mountainsides. Avalanches can travel at 130 miles per hour (209 kilometers per hour). That's twice as fast as a car drives on the highway!

WORDS TO KNOW

plateau: a large, raised area that is fairly flat.

limestone: a sedimentary rock that forms from the skeletons and shells of sea creatures. Limestone erodes easily.

cave: a natural underground opening connected to the surface, large enough for a person to enter.

THE OZARKS

The Ozark Mountains stretch across southern Missouri and northern Arkansas, as well as the eastern corners of Kansas and Oklahoma. These mountains began as a broad, uplifted area that formed a **plateau**. Later, the area was crossed by rivers, which cut valleys into the plateau. The mountains themselves are what used to be the top of the plateau. While the Ozarks are nowhere near as high as the Rockies, they're the largest mountains between the Rockies and the Appalachians in the east. The highest Ozark peak is Turner Ward Knob in Arkansas, which is 2,463 feet tall (751 meters).

The region has large areas of **limestone**, where **caves** and springs have formed. Missouri has over 6,000 caves and is known as the "cave state."

Missouri

Kansas

Oklahoma

Ozark Plateau

Arkansas

MAKE YOUR OWN
FOLDED MOUNTAINS

SUPPLIES

- at least 3 colors of play clay
- rolling pin
- table knife

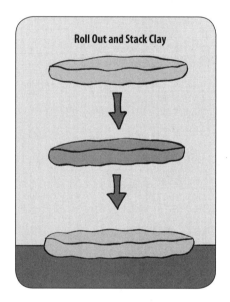

Roll Out and Stack Clay

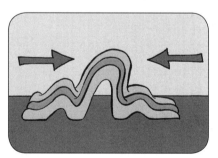

1 Roll out each color of clay into the size and shape of a very large pancake, about ¼ inch thick (½ centimeter). If you have enough clay, roll out extra layers. Stack the layers on top of each other, alternating colors.

2 Place your hands on the outside edges of the stack and gently push towards the middle. The clay should form into 2 or 3 folds. You may have to lift the middle up to help it form the folds. It's okay if the folds flop over a bit on their sides. This is like two tectonic plates colliding and forcing the crust to fold.

3 Rotate the folded clay 90 degrees. Repeat step 2 so that you are folding the folds. You will need to lift the middle to form the second fold. The clay should have rough dome shapes.

30

4 With the table knife, slice off the top ½ inch of the domes (1 centimeter). How do the layers of clay look? Try slicing vertically along one side of the dome. Then try slicing at an angle. This is like the erosion of rocks.

5 Try this again with new clay but experiment with different ways of folding the clay.

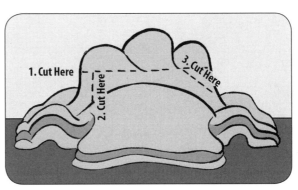

1. Cut Here
2. Cut Here
3. Cut Here

What's Happening?

When tectonic plates are on the move, rocks are often buried at great depths where it's much hotter. When forces act on these hot rocks, they can fold, just like your clay.

Often, rocks get pushed from different directions over time. When that happens, folds in the rocks can get re-folded, which is called superposed folding. This is what happened when you re-folded your clay. Then, when the rocks are later uplifted above the ground and eroded, the folds and rock layers can look different depending on where the erosion happened. The same thing happened when you cut the clay at different angles.

CHAPTER 3

VOLCANOES AND EARTHQUAKES!

The stable interior of the United States doesn't seem like the place for hazards like volcanoes and earthquakes. Have you ever heard of a volcano in Kansas? But if you scratch beneath the surface of the thick soils, you'll find volcanoes and earthquakes with a violent past—and they're still active today!

VOLCANOES!

Volcanoes form when magma comes to the surface. Sometimes this liquid rock cools before it reaches the surface. When that happens, it forms rocks such as granite. But when the magma comes all the way to the surface before it cools, it's called lava. Then it **erupts** through an opening in the earth called a volcano.

The Rocky Mountains contain rocks that were formed from volcanoes that erupted many millions of years ago. Even the Great Plains have volcanic rocks deep beneath the surface. These rocks formed even farther back in the past, when the continent was still being put together.

But if you're interested in seeing active volcanic features, there's only one place to go in the Rockies or Great Plains: Yellowstone!

WORDS TO KNOW

erupt: to burst out suddenly.

hot spring: a natural pool of water that is heated by hot or molten rock. Hot springs are found in areas of volcanic activity.

geyser: a hot spring that periodically ejects water and steam in the air.

thermal: related to heat.

YELLOWSTONE

Bubbling mud pots, gorgeous aqua-blue **hot springs**, and explosive **geysers**. That's what you'll see if you visit Yellowstone National Park. Yellowstone is our nation's oldest National Park, established in 1872.

It has incredible wildlife and scenery, but is best known for its volcanic features. There are 10,000 **thermal** features like geysers and hot springs. This is over half of all the thermal features in the world!

Did You Know?

The tallest active geyser in the world is at Yellowstone National Park. Steamboat Geyser shoots water and steam up to 300 feet high (91 meters)! It's not easy to see, though. The last time Steamboat Geyser erupted was in 2005.

A geyser is a huge fountain of hot water and steam that explodes upward. Around the world, geysers are rare, but Yellowstone is full of them. It has 300 geysers, which is over half of all the geysers in the world. Yellowstone's most famous geyser is called Old Faithful. It's the most regular geyser in the world that is over 100 feet high (30 meters). It erupts about every 90 minutes, shooting up to 8,400 gallons of boiling hot water (32,000 liters) for as long as 5 minutes and as high as 184 feet (56 meters)!

WORDS TO KNOW

mud pot: a boiling area of mud.

fumarole: a vent that lets out hot gases.

How do these volcanic features form? You need three things.

Heat from hot magma that has been brought close to the earth's surface.

Water from rain and snow that has seeped into the earth deep enough to come close to the magma and absorb its heat. Heat and water together produces all sorts of interesting volcanic features, such as **mud pots**, **fumaroles**, and hot springs.

Blockage to create the most unusual thermal feature—a geyser. You

also need a special kind of plumbing system. Geysers have vertical tubes that connect underground areas that store lots of water to the surface. As the water storage areas fill, the tube slowly fills up with heated water and gas bubbles.

In a geyser, the gas bubbles are trapped by a blockage. When the gas bubbles finally break free, they explode upward with the hot water.

This triggers superheated water from below to turn to steam and explode upward, forming a giant, gushing geyser! The system then slowly refills with water, starting the cycle over again.

Yellowstone also has the largest active volcano in the United States, and probably in the world. You may have heard of the eruption in 1980 of Mount St. Helens in Washington State. It killed 57 people and destroyed bridges, railways, trees, and 200 homes.

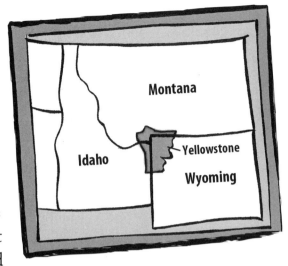

Did You Know?

An active volcano is a volcano that has erupted in recorded history. Geologists think it will erupt again, probably in the next 200 years. A dormant volcano is a "sleepy" volcano that hasn't erupted in recorded history, but could erupt again. An extinct volcano is one that hasn't erupted in many thousands of years and isn't expected to erupt again.

Compared with eruptions from the Yellowstone volcano in Wyoming, Mount St. Helens was a baby. This is a volcano that could produce thousands of times as much ash and lava as most volcanoes.

The Yellowstone volcano is so large and potentially destructive, it's called a supervolcano.

Yellowstone first erupted about 17 million years ago, and has had at least 140 large eruptions. The Yellowstone volcano had three giant eruptions 2 million, 1.3 million, and 642,000 years ago. One produced about 2,500 times more ash than the 1980 eruption of Mount St. Helens. Yellowstone is such a large volcano because it is fed by a huge source of heat. Scientists estimate that the underground plume of hot and partly molten rock that feeds the Yellowstone volcano is about 400 miles long (644 kilometers)!

WORDS TO KNOW

caldera: a large volcanic crater, usually formed by a large eruption that collapses the mouth of the volcano.

Did You Know?

The largest eruption of the Yellowstone volcano produced an ash cloud 10 miles high (16 kilometers). It spewed enough ash to cover half of North America in ash up to 6 feet thick (2 meters).

Instead of the typical cone shape of many volcanoes, the Yellowstone volcano sits on a vast depression, or sunken area. When a volcano with a very large magma chamber erupts, the volcano collapses after all that magma has been expelled. This forms a **caldera** where the magma chamber once was. Yellowstone's caldera is 34 miles by 45 miles (55 by 72 kilometers). It is filled with lakes and hot springs.

Yellowstone is still considered active because of all of its hot springs and geysers, even though it isn't currently erupting with ash and lava. Geologists have been monitoring geologic activity at Yellowstone National Park for over 30 years. They think it will be thousands of years before another major eruption occurs.

WHY IN WYOMING?

Most volcanoes form around the edges of tectonic plates. This is where one plate is subducting beneath another, or where rifting is occurring. Nearly all of the active volcanoes in the Unites States are along its west coast where the Pacific Plate is subducting beneath the North American Plate. Why is Yellowstone, in the middle of the continent, the site of the largest volcano in the United States?

Scientists think the Yellowstone volcano is caused by a hot spot from deep in the earth that is melting rock closer to the surface. Hotspots are small, extremely hot regions beneath the surface of the earth that usually occur in the middle of a plate. As material rises over a hotspot, it melts.

As a volcano moves past the hotspot, that volcano slowly dies out and a new one forms over the hotspot. The North American Plate is moving southwest about 1 inch per year over the Yellowstone hotspot (2½ centimeters). The Yellowstone hotspot first formed beneath where Idaho, Nevada, and Oregon come together. It has migrated slowly to its present location at Yellowstone National Park in northwest Wyoming.

EARTHQUAKES!

Have you ever felt an earthquake? When stress builds up in rocks, they can suddenly lurch into a new position. That lurching is called an earthquake. Most earthquakes happen along faults, which are cracks in the outer layer of the earth.

WORDS TO KNOW

seismic wave: a wave of energy generated from an earthquake. The wave travels through the earth.

When an earthquake occurs, it releases huge amounts of energy. Waves of energy travel out in all directions as **seismic waves**. It's a bit like tossing a large rock into a pond. The ripples of water spread out in all directions.

Stress Builds in Rocks Along Fault Line

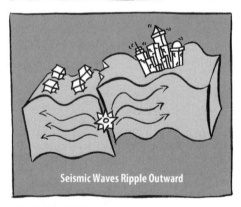

Earthquake: Rocks Lurch Into New Position

Seismic Waves Ripple Outward

Plates Come to Rest in Position

Faults don't open up and there's no giant hole you can fall into when an earthquake occurs. An earthquake is movement that happens along the fault. In fact, the whole reason an earthquake occurs is because faults get "locked up" due to friction. In an earthquake, the two sides of the fault lurch into a new position. If the fault opened up, there would be no friction. Sometimes there can be a shallow opening in the earth after an earthquake because of a landslide.

NEW MADRID SEISMIC ZONE

Do you know which state in the United States had the earthquake that affected the largest area in recorded history? Do you think of California? It's true that California has lots of earthquakes. But the earthquake that affected the largest area happened in the center of the United States, in New Madrid, Missouri.

The New Madrid seismic zone is a system of faults right in the middle of the North American Plate. The area is where Missouri, Kentucky, Arkansas, and Tennessee meet. There are several faults here about 150 miles long (241 kilometers), from Arkansas to southern Illinois.

In 1811 and 1812, there were three huge earthquakes along these faults that measured 7.5 to 8.0 on the **Richter scale**. Since they happened before there were modern instruments to measure earthquakes, scientists have to estimate their strength based on newspaper reports and looking at changes in the rocks.

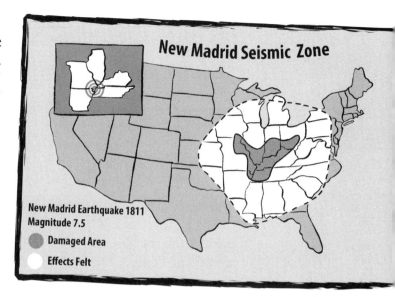

New Madrid Earthquake 1811 Magnitude 7.5
Damaged Area
Effects Felt

These were the largest quakes east of the Rocky Mountains in recorded history. They were felt farther than much larger ones in Alaska because the older, colder rocks in the craton transmit seismic waves farther. People felt them from the Rocky Mountains to the Atlantic Ocean and from Canada to Mexico.

WORDS TO KNOW

Richter scale: a scale used to measure the strength of an earthquake.

seismograph: an instrument that measures the intensity of a seismic wave.

Sidewalks buckled in Baltimore, Maryland. Chimneys fell down in Cincinnati, Ohio. Church bells rang in Boston, Massachusetts.

In Washington, D.C., President James Madison and his wife Dolly thought someone was robbing the White House. And the banks on the Mississippi River collapsed. In some places the earth tilted so much that the river ran backwards for awhile!

Will another "Big One" happen? The only question is when. Each year there are about 500,000 earthquakes that are detectable by **seismographs**. About 100,000 of them can be felt by humans. About 100 of them cause damage. In the area of New Madrid, there are earthquakes on most days, but usually you can't feel them.

HOW BIG IS THAT EARTHQUAKE?

Earthquakes are measured mainly by their magnitude. Magnitude is the strength of an earthquake and is recorded on the Richter scale. When the measurement increases by 1, the magnitude increases by 10. So an earthquake that measures 8.0 is 10 times as powerful as an earthquake that measures 7.0. Here are some typical effects that people might feel near the epicenter of earthquakes of various magnitudes. This is the point on the earth's surface directly above the location of the earthquake.

Magnitude on the Richter Scale	What it Feels Like	How Often They Occur in the World
Below 3.0	You usually can't feel it.	1,000 per day
3.0 to 3.9	You can feel a slight trembling, but there is no damage.	Over 100 per day
4.0 to 4.9	Tables and chairs rattle.	About 20 per day
5.0 to 6.9	Some damage to buildings, especially if they're poorly built.	About 3 per day
7.0 to 7.9	Serious damage to buildings, with some destroyed.	18 per year
8.0 to 8.9	Serious damage for several hundred miles.	1 per year
9.0 to 9.9	Devastating, affecting people for thousands of miles.	1 per 20 years
10.0 and up	Never recorded.	?

The New Madrid area has experienced major earthquakes over the past 65 million years, but only once every million years or so. That rate seems to be speeding up lately. The last 2,000 years have had between two and four major earthquakes.

Scientists think there may be more frequent earthquakes because of changing pressures on the crust from melting glaciers in the last 18,000 years. They think a major earthquake is 100 or more years off, but a smaller, still dangerous earthquake of perhaps magnitude 6.0 will probably happen sooner. This would damage bridges and buildings.

BIG EARTHQUAKES IN THE PAST

A significant earthquake usually leaves a record in the rocks. Geologists can read that record, just like you would read a book. They look closely at faults that have moved in the past 10,000 years. These are the best predictors of when and where earthquakes might occur in the future. What do geologists look for?

Paleoliquefaction is evidence of liquefaction that has occurred in the past. Liquefaction is when soil flows like a liquid, usually due to a large earthquake. The vibrations from the earthquake loosen the water-filled soil and break the grain-to-grain contact. Sometimes sand "boils" when the liquefied sand bursts through surface clay and spills onto the earth's surface.

The New Madrid earthquakes produced lots of sand boils. This is because, over millions of years, the Mississippi River has deposited huge amounts of sand covered over by clay. Scientists can see these circular areas of sand boils using pictures taken from the air.

Did You Know?

The largest recorded earthquake in the world was in Chile on May 22, 1960. It measured 9.5 on the Richter scale. Seismographs all over the world recorded the seismic waves for several days. The entire earth was shaking!

WHY IN MISSOURI AND ARKANSAS?

Like volcanoes, most earthquakes occur near the edges of plates. For example, the famous San Andreas fault system in California occurs where two plates grind past each other. The massive earthquake in Japan in March 2011 that caused the devastating tsunami was also the result of plates moving past each other. Other earthquakes can occur as one plate subducts beneath another.

The New Madrid seismic zone is in the middle of the North American Plate, but it's still affected by the movement of plates. Scientists think that about 500 million years ago, the continent starting rifting apart there. Even though the rifting stopped, the crust is still weak in this area. The faults that formed from the rifting were later covered by sediments. But they're like a scar buried under the sediments that hasn't completely healed. When pressure builds from movements in the earth, these old faults are places that are weaker, so earthquakes occur there.

Stalagmites are another clue. These are cave formations that scientists can study to date an earthquake. Stalagmites grow slowly into cone-shaped formations when drips of water filled with minerals fall on the ground of a cave and slowly build up.

If the earth moves in an earthquake, the source of the drip moves too. That makes the growth of the stalagmite shift, and you can see where it changes. Scientists cut paper-thin slices where the change happened and analyze the minerals to tell when the crystals formed. This is the date of the earthquake.

Did You Know?

A United States Geological Survey web site shows earthquakes over the last seven days for the United States. Go to http://earthquake.usgs.gov/earthquakes/. There are usually dots for earthquakes around the "boot heel" in the southeast corner of Missouri for the New Madrid seismic zone.

MAKE YOUR OWN
LIQUEFACTION

1 Fill the bowl about halfway with ice cubes. Place the stick into the ice cubes so that it is vertical and standing on its own.

2 Using the pitcher, slowly pour water into the bowl. Stop when the water level is below the top of the ice cubes. Is the stick still vertical?

3 Continue filling the bowl with water until the ice cubes float. Is the stick still vertical?

SUPPLIES

- large bowl
- ice cubes, enough to fill the bowl halfway
- short stick
- cold water
- cup or pitcher

What's Happening?

When loose, sandy soil is saturated with water, the water fills the gaps between the grains of sand. Under normal conditions the grains still touch each other so the sand is firm and can support buildings. This is like when the water was below the top of the ice cubes. When an earthquake occurs, the shaking puts pressure on the water and the sand becomes briefly suspended in the water. The grains are no longer touching each other and they can't support objects. This is called liquefaction, because the sandy soil behaves like a liquid. Buildings can tilt or sink into the squishy soil. In your experiment, when there was enough water for the ice cubes to float, the cubes no longer touched each other, and they couldn't hold up the stick.

MAKE YOUR OWN GEYSER

1 Roll one of the index cards into a tube as wide as the opening of the bottle. Place tape around the tube at the top and bottom, leaving both ends open. Open the bottle of soda and set it on the ground outside so it is stable and doesn't tip over.

2 Stack the Mentos in the index-card tube. Place the second index card on top of the tube and turn the tube upside down. Place both on top of the opening of the bottle so that the tube is just over the opening, with the flat index card in between.

3 Pull out the index card and let the Mentos slide into the soda. Stand back!

SUPPLIES

- 2 index cards
- cellophane tape
- 2-liter bottle of soda
- roll of Mentos candy

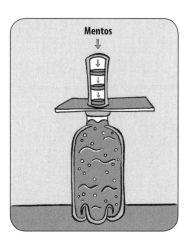

What's Happening?

Soda is bubbly because it contains gases dissolved in water. This gas was dissolved into the soda at the factory under high pressure. When you open a bottle of soda, it reduces the pressure and allows bubbles to form. Adding the Mentos helps the bubbles form much faster. They form so fast they explode upward out of the bottle, taking lots of soda with them. When hot water and gas come near the earth's surface, they form hot springs. But sometimes the pathway is blocked and the pressure builds up like when the cap is on a soda bottle. When the water and gas finally break through the blockage, they explode in a fountain of hot water and steam.

CHAPTER 4

THE PLAINS

From the Rocky Mountains in the west to the Appalachian Mountains in the east, the Plains spread farther than you can see. These vast expanses of flat land are the heart of America, covered in grass and fields of corn and wheat.

OLD ROCKS AND A NEW SHAPE

The central part of the United States contains its oldest rocks, dating back to long before the rest of the country existed. The Plains are part of the North American Craton, where rocks are hundreds of millions of years old. Some rocks in northern Minnesota are between 3.5 and 3.7 billion years old!

WORDS TO KNOW

acidic: from acids, which are chemical compounds that taste sour.

carbon dioxide: a gas formed by the rotting of plants and animals and when animals breathe out.

carbonic acid: a weak acid formed when carbon dioxide dissolves in water.

Most of the craton was covered by a thin, flat layer of younger sedimentary rocks when a shallow sea swept into the interior part of the country. The sea advanced and receded many times. Because there hasn't been mountain-forming tectonic activity in this region since then, the region has remained relatively flat. In much more recent times, glaciers moved into the Northern Plains and carved the surface of the land.

LOOK OUT BELOW: CAVES!

The Plains have thousands of caves of all shapes and sizes. Some are just a shallow hollow in the earth, while others wind for tens or even hundreds of miles in total darkness. Most of them are limestone caves.

Thick layers of limestone were deposited when a shallow sea covered the interior of North America.

Limestone is a type of rock that dissolves in slightly **acidic** water. Lemon juice and vinegar are acids, so if you added a few drops of lemon juice to water it would be slightly acidic. Taste plain lemon juice and the acid in it will make your mouth pucker! All rainfall is naturally slightly acidic because **carbon dioxide** in the air reacts with water to form **carbonic acid**.

WORDS TO KNOW

cavern: a very large cave or system of connected caves.

Limestone often has cracks in it, and rainwater seeps into these cracks. The carbonic acid in the rainwater slowly dissolves the rock, making the cracks wider. In some caves, a stream can travel through the limestone until it finds an outlet, eroding even more rock along the way. Eventually, part of the roof can collapse, which forms larger **caverns**. There are many caverns in the Plains that began forming not long after the inland sea receded and limestone was exposed.

JEWEL CAVE

Jewel Cave in South Dakota is one of the most beautiful caves in the world. It's also the second longest. So far, cavers have explored 155 miles (249 kilometers) of the cave, but they aren't finished. Based on studies done with movements of air, scientists think it is thousands of miles long!

Mixed in with the limestone is another mineral, called gypsum. The seeping rainwater picks up bits of gypsum, which it then deposits in the caves. Gypsum formations are very delicate, and they form only in dry parts of the cave. This is because gypsum dissolves so easily in water. Jewel Cave has gypsum crystals that are formed like flowers, needles, beards, and spiders. You can visit Jewel Cave and see these amazing formations for yourself!

WORDS TO KNOW

speleothem: a distinctive cave formation, such as a stalactite.

stalactite: a cave formation that looks like an icicle hanging from the ceiling.

stalagmite: a cave formation that sticks up from the floor, often under a stalactite.

CAVE FORMATIONS

Once caverns form, cave formations of all shapes and sizes can develop that look like teeth, columns, curtains, pearls, and beards! These cave formations are called **speleothems**. As rainwater seeps through limestone and dissolves it, the limestone doesn't disappear—it's just in the water. When water drips from the ceiling of a cave, a very small bit of limestone is left behind. Drop by drop, huge speleothems form. Maybe you've seen pictures of **stalactites** and **stalagmites**.

The kind of speleothem formed depends mainly on whether the water drips, trickles, or seeps into the cave.

- **Stalactites** grow where water drips from the ceiling.

- **Stalagmites** grow where water drips onto the floor.

- **Draperies** grow where water runs down a slanted ceiling or wall.

- **Columns** are where a stalactite and stalagmite meet.

- **Soda straws** are hollow tubes that grow where water seeps through the ceiling. They can turn into a stalactite if the hole at the bottom gets blocked.

- **Pearls** grow in pools of calcite-rich water like an oyster pearl. They grow layer upon layer around a grain of sand.

- **Flowstone** grows where water flows over walls or floors.

- **Beards** are clumps of delicate, thin threads that grow from water containing dissolved gypsum.

- **Popcorn** formations are clusters that look like popcorn or grapes. They are found on ceilings, floors, and walls of caves.

SOME FAMOUS CAVES OF THE MIDWEST

Bear Cave, Michigan: named for skeletons of the extinct cave bear.

Bluespring Caverns, Indiana: contains the longest known underground river in the United States. It is 3 miles long (5 kilometers).

Bridal Cave, Missouri: where over 2,000 couples have married.

Cave of the Mounds, Wisconsin: its huge variety of speleothems include soda straws, flowstones, and cave pearls.

Cave of the Winds, Colorado: its rare crystalline speleothems include cave flowers.

Fantastic Caverns, Missouri: has a tour through the entire cavern in a tram.

Illinois Caverns, Illinois: many of its formations are still actively growing.

Marengo Cave, Indiana: discovered in 1883 by two children, Orris and Blanche Hiestand, ages 11 and 15.

Did You Know?

The longest known cave is Mammoth Cave in Kentucky with a length of 390 miles (628 kilometers). It's also one of the oldest tourist attractions in the United States. People have been going on tours of Mammoth Cave since 1816.

WORDS TO KNOW

species: a group of plants or animals that are related and look the same.

Minnetonka Cave, Idaho: five different **species** of bats hibernate in it.

Ohio Caverns, Ohio: with the colorful Jewel Room that has been called "America's Most Colorful Cavern."

Wind Cave, South Dakota: known for its boxwork, which is an unusual speleothem made of thin fins that look like honeycombs. Wind Cave is near Jewel Cave, and the two caves may be connected deep underground. It is one of the world's longest and oldest caves.

GLACIERS: MASTER SCULPTORS

Most of the northern plains have been transformed by the action of glaciers. How did glaciers come so far south, and why aren't they here now? First let's look at glaciers and how they form.

When more snow falls than melts each year, it accumulates and eventually forms a glacier.

Snowflakes have a beautiful crystal structure that is often six-sided. At first, when snow falls, it's light and fluffy. About 80 percent of it is air. Over time, the snowflakes lose air and compress, becoming **granules**. After about a year, only 50 percent is air and it's called **firn**. With even more time, the firn melts slightly and refreezes and even more air is squeezed out. The snowflakes have become glacial ice.

Glaciers thicken where more snow accumulates. This is called the **zone of accumulation**. When the ice grows thick enough it begins to move from the force of **gravity**.

Snow Flake Granular Snow Firn Glacier Ice

A glacier moves in two ways. The thin layer of melted water at the base of a glacier helps it slide along the ground. But it can also move from the inside. Because of the great weight of glaciers, pressure causes the ice crystals deep inside a glacier to line up into layers. These layers slide against each other like a deck of cards. The ice can actually bend and flow, a bit like Silly Putty. Sometimes glaciers even have folds inside. As a glacier moves downhill, it melts where it's warmer. The area where the glacier melts is called the **zone of ablation**.

WORDS TO KNOW

zone of ablation: the area on a glacier where snow or ice melts or evaporates.

When more snow falls at the zone of accumulation than melts in the zone of ablation, the glacier grows. When less snow falls than melts, the glacier shrinks.

There are two main types of glaciers: alpine and continental.

Alpine glaciers are formed in valleys high in the mountains where temperatures are colder. The Rocky Mountains have alpine glaciers.

Continental glaciers are huge ice sheets that completely cover the land of a major part of a continent. Today, there are continental glaciers on Greenland and Antarctica. But in the past, continental glaciers covered much of northern North America and northern Europe and Asia.

Did You Know?

It actually takes longer to form glacial ice in very cold temperatures. That's because it's so cold that snow doesn't melt enough to refreeze into solid ice very quickly. A glacier in Alaska might take 30 to 50 years to form. But in Antarctica, where it's extremely cold, it might take as long as 3,500 years!

WORDS TO KNOW

Pleistocene: the epoch in geologic history from about 2.5 million years ago to 10,000 years ago that experienced repeated glaciations.

Ice Age: a period of time when large ice sheets cover large areas of land. It particularly refers to the most recent series of glaciations during the Pleistocene. An ice age can include shorter periods when glaciers retreat, as well as periods when the glaciers grow.

glacial period: a period of time within an ice age when a large part of the earth's surface is covered with ice.

interglacial period: a period within an ice age that is somewhat warmer and glaciers retreat.

ICE AGE!

Earth's climate goes through natural variations in temperature over time. This is due to a complex interaction of the distance from the sun, how Earth turns on its axis, and where the continents are.

In the last 2.5 million years, until about 10,000 years ago, there have been at least 11 major cycles of cooling and warming. This entire time is called the **Pleistocene**, or sometimes just the **Ice Age**. During the cold periods, temperatures dropped over many, many years and glaciers expanded. These are called **glacial periods**.

During the warmer periods, called **interglacial periods**, the glaciers shrank. During the glacial periods of the Ice Age, about 30 percent of the land on Earth was covered in ice up to 2 miles thick (3 kilometers).

In North America, ice covered the northern part of the Midwest and extended as far south as southern Illinois and central Missouri.

The most recent glacial period began about 100,000 years ago. It is called the Wisconsin Glacial Episode because you can see its effects best in the state of Wisconsin. Some of the key discoveries and the first map of the extent of glaciation in North America were made in southeastern Wisconsin.

The Wisconsin glaciation lasted until about 10,000 years ago. During glaciations, the sea level falls because water is held in the glaciers. During the Wisconsin glaciation the sea level fell enough to expose land linking Asia and Alaska and created a "land bridge." Many scientists think that humans and animals migrated across this bridge from Asia into North America sometime between 12,000 and 20,000 years ago. From Alaska, people then migrated throughout the Americas.

No one knows whether the Ice Age is over or still going on. Interglacial periods last about 10,000 to 12,000 years, and we've been in an interglacial period for about that long. Human effects on the climate could possibly delay the start of another glacial period.

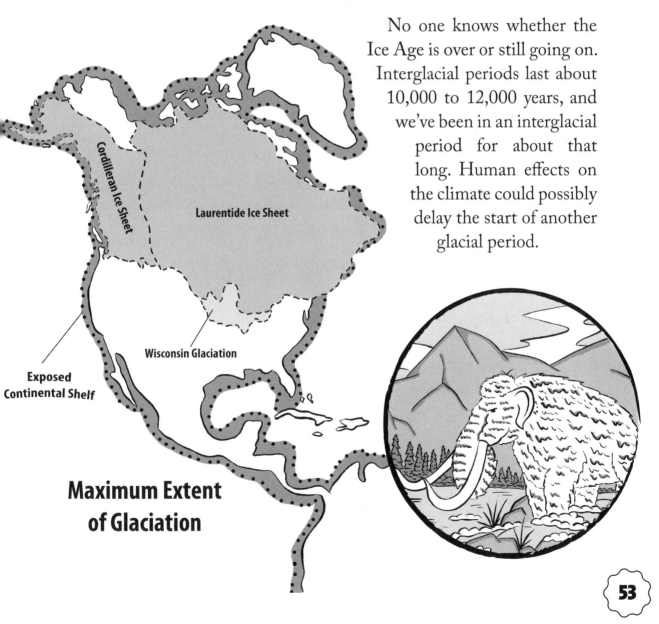

Cordilleran Ice Sheet

Laurentide Ice Sheet

Wisconsin Glaciation

Exposed Continental Shelf

Maximum Extent of Glaciation

GLACIAL LAND FORMS

Glaciers erode the land and reshape it. When glaciers move, their great weight cracks and crushes the rock beneath. The glacier plucks up chunks of rock and carries them along. These chunks can vary in size from fine sediment called **rock flour** to house-sized boulders. They are frozen into the ice and, as they move, the rock chunks grind and polish the bedrock underneath—a bit like sandpaper.

When the glacier melts, it deposits this material into various landforms.

Many of these effects of glaciers might be hard to recognize because the landforms are covered over by **grasslands**, forests, and fields. But look beyond the vegetation and you might see some clues that a glacier has been around.

Scratches and grooves in the bedrock: these are deep parallel scratches where the glacier scraped over ground carrying broken rock.

Glacial polish: just like you might polish brass with cleaner that has a bit of grit in it, glaciers with rock flour polish the underlying bedrock. The rock has a smooth surface, almost like glass.

Esker: when a glacier has a river flowing underneath it, that river deposits material just like regular rivers do. When the entire glacier melts, the deposited material forms a meandering ridge of till called an esker.

Did You Know?

Ice is a type of metamorphic rock, which is rock that has been changed by temperature and pressure. It just happens to have a lower melting point than any other rock.

Till: a random mixture of clay, rocks, and gravel, which is carried along by a glacier and then deposited as the ice melts.

Moraines: deposits of till that form on the sides and front of glaciers. As the glacier melts, the till is dropped out into mounds and ridges. Terminal moraines trace the farthest edge of a glacier.

Erratic: a rock that has been carried by a glacier from another location. Erratics can be as small as a pebble or as large as a house. Scientists try to determine where erratics came from to help them map the flow directions of the glacier. You can find numerous erratics throughout Voyageurs National Park. One erratic in Alberta, Canada weighs over 18,000 tons (16,329 metric tons)!

Did You Know?

Twice in the long-ago past—710 and 635 million years ago—scientists believe Earth was covered in ice sheets, even at the equator! Scientists call this the Snowball Earth Theory. Even during this deep freeze, life survived in the form of tiny, single-celled microbes.

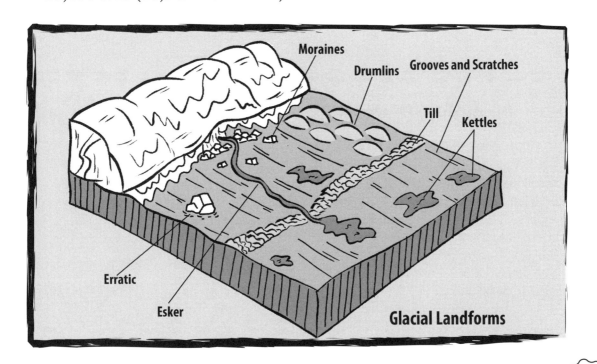

Moraines — Drumlins — Grooves and Scratches — Till — Kettles — Erratic — Esker

Glacial Landforms

Did You Know?

Minnesota is called the Land of 10,000 Lakes, although it has even more than that. Most of those lakes formed when water filled in kettles left by retreating glaciers.

Drumlin: a smooth, teardrop-shaped mound that was molded by a glacier. These often occur in groups and from above can look like a pod of whales swimming. You can find drumlins at Isle Royale National Park, an island in Lake Superior.

Kettle: a bowl-shaped depression. Kettles form when a block of ice is separated from the glacier and is covered by till. When the ice later melts, the till collapses into a bowl shape. In southeast Wisconsin, Kettle Moraine is an area with numerous kettles. They are often filled with water, creating lakes and ponds. The kettles formed where two **lobes** of the glacier met and large blocks of ice broke off.

WORDS TO KNOW

lobe: an extension of a glacier, with a shape like a tongue. The Wisconsin glaciation had six major lobes.

ICE AGE NATIONAL SCENIC TRAIL

The Ice Age National Scenic Trail covers 1,200 miles through Wisconsin (1,931 kilometers). It traces the edge of the Wisconsin glaciation, highlighting landscape features from the Ice Age. You can see moraines, eskers, erratics, kettles, drumlins, and more—probably better than anywhere else on Earth! Other national parks where you can find evidence of glaciation in the Midwest are Voyageurs National Park in Minnesota and Isle Royale National Park in Michigan.

Did You Know?

Glaciers often have a bluish or greenish tint because most of the air has been squeezed out.

56

MAKE YOUR OWN
KETTLES

SUPPLIES

- shallow pan
- sand or dirt
- ice cubes
- water

1 Fill the pan about ½ inch deep with sand (1 centimeter). Set several ice cubes into the sand with at least 2 inches between cubes (5 centimeters).

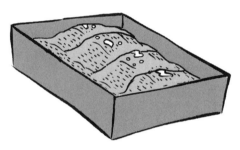

2 Fill in the spaces between the cubes with sand. Keep adding sand until it covers the ice cubes with about ¼ inch of sand (½ centimeter). The top of the sand should be level. Sprinkle water on the sand until it's damp.

3 Wait an hour or so. What does the surface of the sand look like? Try slowly adding more water. Does it fill the holes?

What's Happening?

The ice cubes are like pieces of a glacier that has broken off. The sand is like the till covering the pieces of glacier. When the block of glacier melts, the till collapses to form a bowl or depression in the land. These are called kettles, and they often fill with water to form lakes and ponds.

MAKE YOUR OWN
NEEDLE-LIKE CRYSTALS

1 Cut the paper into whatever shape you like, such as a snowflake or heart. Place the paper on the cookie sheet. The paper needs to fit completely within the cookie sheet.

2 Slowly pour the Epsom salts into the hot water, stirring constantly. Keep stirring until all of the Epsom salts are dissolved, if possible. Add food coloring if you like.

3 Pour the solution over the paper. Place the cookie sheet with the paper and solution in a warm place, like a sunny window. With an adult's help, you can also place the cookie sheet in a warm oven (200 degrees Fahrenheit/93 degrees Celsius) for 15 minutes or so, but watch it to make sure it doesn't dry out too much. You should start to see lots of large, spiky crystals growing.

SUPPLIES

- black cardstock or construction paper
- scissors
- shallow cookie sheet or pie pan
- 1 cup Epsom salts from the pharmacy (240 grams)
- 1 cup hot tap water (250 milliliters)
- spoon
- food coloring (optional)

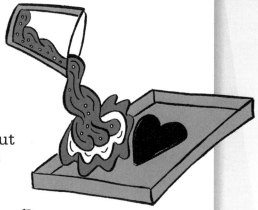

What's Happening?

Like limestone and gypsum, epsomite is a mineral that dissolves in water. It has an appearance that looks like long threads. Epsomite can be found on the walls of some limestone caves, such as Marengo Cave in Indiana.

CHAPTER 5

CLIMATE

The Great Plains are home to some of the most violent storms on Earth. Far from the oceans, the plains and mountains are often a battleground between big movements of cold and warm air. This makes for extremes in temperatures and huge storms. Let's take a look around the region to find out why it has such interesting weather. But hold onto your hat—it's windy out there!

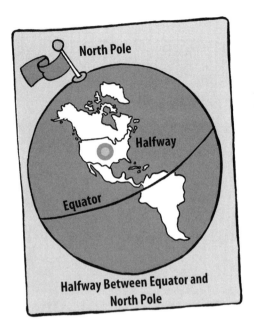

North Pole

Halfway

Equator

Halfway Between Equator and North Pole

continental climate: the climate found in the middle of a continent. It is characterized by large variations in temperature and four seasons.

HOT, HOT, HOT . . . THEN COLD, COLD

If you could stand in the middle of the Great Plains with no limits on how far you could see, you would notice a few things. First, you're about halfway between the equator and the North Pole. This is called a temperate zone. It means that the weather varies quite a bit from season to season, with both hot and cold weather.

Next, you'd notice that you're far from any oceans. What does that have to do with climate? Water heats up and cools down more slowly than rock or soil or plants. The temperatures of large bodies of water like the oceans don't change as much between winter and summer as land does. So areas near oceans doesn't have as many extremes in temperature, especially if winds tend to blow from the ocean onto the land.

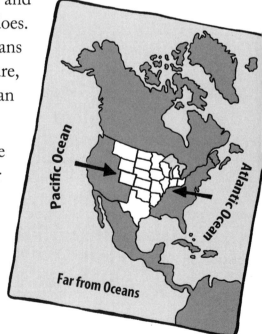

Pacific Ocean

Atlantic Ocean

Far from Oceans

But regions far from oceans have large variations in temperature between summer and winter. The Midwest has the largest annual temperature variations outside of Alaska. Even though winters can be deeply cold, summers can also be blistering hot. This is called a **continental climate**.

WORDS TO KNOW

tornado: a violent, twisting, funnel-shaped column of air extending from a thunderstorm to the ground.

blizzard: a severe snow storm with high winds, low temperatures, and heavy snow.

Which city would you guess has had the hottest temperature: Miami, Florida, or Bismarck, North Dakota? Are you surprised that Miami has never recorded temperatures above 100 degrees Fahrenheit (38 degrees Celsius)? Bismarck, on the other hand, reached 114 degrees Fahrenheit in July 1936 (45 degrees Celsius). But on average, North Dakota is the second-coldest state, right behind Alaska. How can this be true? Look on a map and see how far each city is from the ocean.

Finally, you'd notice that for a long way, the land is very flat. To the east you'd see the Appalachian Mountains, and to the west you'd see the Rocky Mountains rising sharply from the plains. The way the mountains and plains are arranged affects the movement of large bodies of air. It makes the region the home of large thunderstorms, **tornadoes**, and **blizzards**.

TEMPERATURE EXTREMES

International Falls, Minnesota, located in the far north of the state, is called "The Icebox of the Nation." It can get mighty cold, with a record low temperature of -58 degrees Fahrenheit (-50 degrees Celsius). With temperatures that cold, you might think it never warms up. But with its continental climate, International Falls has a record high temperature of 103 degrees Fahrenheit (39 degrees Celsius). The difference in average temperatures between summer and winter there is almost 89 degrees Fahrenheit (31 degrees Celsius).

STORM COMING THROUGH!

Have you ever heard someone say that a storm front is coming into the area? A large, moving pocket of air is called an air mass. When a warm, moist air mass collides with a cold, dry air mass, the area where they meet is called a front. Storms often occur along fronts because the air there is unstable.

Did You Know?

A blizzard stormed across Minnesota, Wisconsin, Michigan, Nebraska, and South Dakota on November 11, 1940. Winds of 80 miles per hour (129 kilometers) drifted snow as high as 20 feet (6 meters)!

In the Midwest, warm, moist air sweeps in from the Gulf of Mexico in the south because there are no mountains to block the air. Colder, dry air comes in from the north and west. When these two air systems meet, look out! In the winter, snowstorms can quickly turn into blizzards. In the summer, towering thunderstorms form, sometimes spawning destructive tornadoes.

SOME EVIL NOVEMBER WITCHES

In the fall, the Great Lakes still have heat, since these large bodies of water cool down more slowly than the surrounding land. The heat adds power to snowstorms, fueling high winds and waves. Sometimes, two or more storms collide over the Great Lakes and form a super storm, especially in the late fall. When this happens it's called a "November witch." Two especially bad ones were the following:

- A November storm in 1975 sank a huge freighter called the *SS Edmund Fitzgerald* on Lake Superior. All of the crew died. It's the largest ship to have sunk in the Great Lakes, measuring 730 feet long (222 meters). Gordon Lightfoot commemorated the sinking in a 1976 hit song "The Wreck of the Edmund Fitzgerald."

- A blizzard raged across the Great Lakes from November 7 to November 10, 1913. The storm had winds of 60 to 90 miles per hour (97 to 145 kilometers) and waves over 35 feet high (11 meters). It destroyed 19 ships and caused over 250 deaths.

WORDS TO KNOW

jet stream: a high-speed flow of air high in the atmosphere that flows from west to east and often brings weather with it.

BLIZZARD!

A blizzard is an intense snowstorm with very low temperatures, lots of blowing snow, and high winds. These storms often bunch up around the Rocky Mountains or track over the Great Lakes.

The **jet stream** is another reason the Midwest gets intense winter temperatures and storms. It has nothing to do with planes, but a jet stream does travel fast. These narrow currents of air high above the surface of the earth travel as fast as 250 miles per hour (400 kilometers).

Weather systems, such as storms, often follow jet streams, which act like a "highway" for storms. Jet streams also follow boundaries between warm and cold air. There's a jet stream above Canada that travels from west to east most of the time. It meanders north and south like a river, but is usually to the north. In the winter the jet stream moves south, bringing with it cold, dry air from the Arctic.

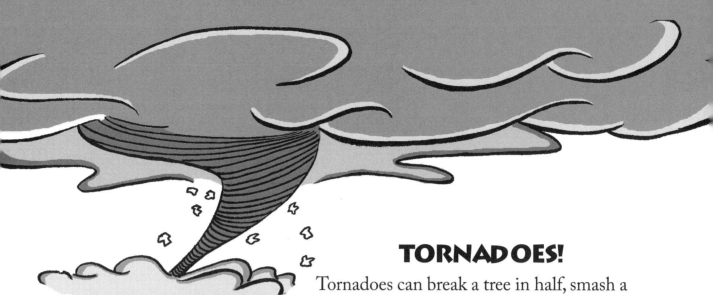

TORNADOES!

Tornadoes can break a tree in half, smash a house, or even move a train down the tracks! They are the most violent storms on Earth. Inside a tornado, winds twist upward in a funnel-shaped column anywhere from 90 to 300 miles per hour (145 to 483 kilometers per hour)! Tornadoes are most likely to occur in the United States in the months of April, May, and June, in the heat of the late afternoon. About 1,000 tornadoes are reported each year.

Tornadoes occur all over the world, but there are more tornadoes in the United States than in any other country.

WORDS TO KNOW

wind shear: a change in the direction of wind, especially when wind blows in different directions at different heights.

supercell: a severe thunderstorm with strong updrafts and downdrafts of air. Supercells often have large hail, strong winds, downpours, and sometimes tornadoes.

condense: to change from a gas to a liquid.

A tornado, also called a twister, often travels in a curved path, and it can be hard to predict which way it will go next. It usually moves over land at about 30 miles per hour or less (48 kilometers), but sometimes faster. It can last for only a few seconds, or for hours. Tornadoes can look like a thin needle or a bowl. Each one is different, but they're all powerful and potentially dangerous.

HOW DO TORNADOES FORM?

A tornado starts with **wind shear**. This is when the wind blows in different directions at different heights. For example, the wind at the ground might be moving north, while the wind higher up is moving south. This difference rolls the air in between into a spinning tube, much like you roll clay between your hands. There can be a lot of wind shear in late spring, making this the "high" season for tornadoes.

Wind shear by itself won't create a tornado. It needs lots of energy too. This can come from a huge, powerful thunderstorm—the kind with dark, almost black clouds, lightning, and sometimes hail. These large thunderstorms, called **supercells**, form when warm, moist air slams into cold, dry air. The moist air rises through the cold air, and as it cools, the moisture **condenses** and forms clouds. As more warm air rises and pumps energy into the system, the clouds turn into thunderstorms.

The rising air in the thunderstorm lifts the tube of spinning air into the storm. When the twisting tube of air tightens and spins down to touch the earth, a tornado is born.

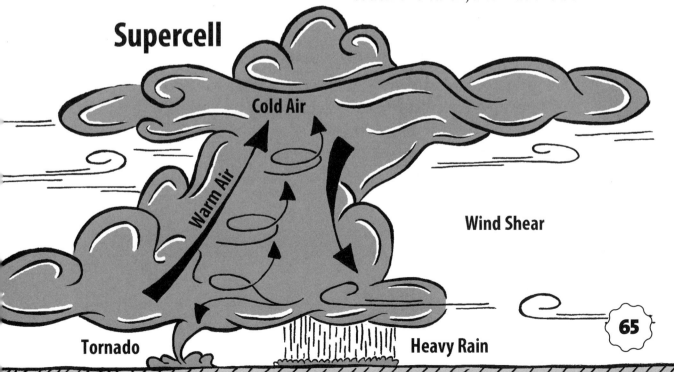

Supercell

Cold Air

Warm Air

Wind Shear

Tornado

Heavy Rain

HOW BAD IS IT?

Tornadoes are rated on a scale called the **Enhanced Fujita scale**. It is named after Theodore Fujita, who first developed a similar scale. The Enhanced Fujita scale was implemented in 2007 and runs from EF-0 to EF-5. Scientists usually can't measure the speed of the winds within most tornadoes, but they can estimate the wind speed based on the damage a tornado causes.

Scale	Wind Speed	Typical Damage
EF-0	65 to 85 mph (105 to 137 kph)	Tree limbs and chimneys broken, some roofs damaged
EF-1	86 to 110 mph (138 to 177 kph)	Roofs peeled off, windows broken, cars overturned
EF-2	111 to 136 mph (179 to 219 kph)	Roofs completely torn off, large trees uprooted, cars lifted off ground, mobile homes destroyed, foundations of homes shifted
EF-3	137 to 165 mph (221 to 267 kph)	Parts of houses and large buildings destroyed, trains overturned, large cars thrown
EF-4	166 to 200 mph (269 to 322 kph)	Houses flattened, cars and structures thrown great distances
EF-5	Greater than 200 mph (324 kph)	Complete destruction with houses swept away and completely destroyed, high-rise buildings badly damaged, cars lifted so they fly through the air, trains lifted off tracks

TORNADO ALLEY

The Midwest has more tornadoes than any other region in the United States because of its intense supercell thunderstorms and wind shear. And where there's a supercell thunderstorm, there's a good chance it will spin out a twister!

The middle part of America is called Tornado Alley because it has so many tornadoes. This area doesn't have an exact definition, but generally includes most of the states of South Dakota, Iowa, Nebraska, Kansas, Oklahoma, Texas, parts of Colorado, and Minnesota. But some people also include other states, from Michigan to Louisiana and east to Ohio. Florida also has many tornadoes, but they are not as intense.

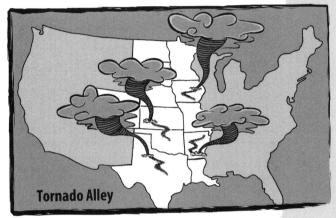

Tornado Alley

WHAT TO DO
WHEN THERE IS A TORNADO

When the weather forecast warns of tornadoes, you need to pay attention. Listen to the radio or TV for more information. And look for signs of big thunderstorms, like a very dark, often greenish sky or large **hail**. If there is a tornado warning, be prepared to take shelter. This means finding a sturdy structure, preferably with a basement. Don't stay in a mobile home. A low-lying, dark cloud that might be swirling or a loud roar are strong warning signs that a tornado is coming.

67

KILLER TORNADOES

These were some of the most powerful and devastating tornadoes:

Super Outbreak: The largest outbreak of tornadoes recorded in one 24-hour period occurred from April 3 to April 4, 1974, called the Super Outbreak. There were 148 documented tornadoes in 13 states on that day. Many of these tornadoes were violent. There were six F5 tornadoes and 24 F4 tornadoes (measured on the original Fujita Scale). Altogether, 330 people were killed and 6,142 were injured by the tornadoes.

The Tri-State Tornado: On March 18, 1925, the single deadliest tornado in United States history killed 695 people. It tore through Missouri, Illinois, and Indiana, leaving 15,000 homes destroyed. In the town of Gorham, Illinois, every single building was destroyed.

WORDS TO KNOW

meteorologist: a scientist who studies and forecasts climate and weather.

The Greensburg Tornado: On May 4, 2007, this tornado completely destroyed the town of Greensburg, Kansas. Luckily, **meteorologists** were able to give residents a 20-minute warning using tornado sirens, so people could get to shelter underground. But hail fell the size of golf balls and winds over 200 miles per hour roared like a jet engine (322 kilometers per hour). The Greensburg Tornado crushed nearly every building in the town.

If you're near a safe structure (a well-built home, school, or hospital) get inside immediately. Go to a basement if possible. Otherwise go to the first floor, as far away from windows as possible, like in a hall or inside closet. Do not open windows. Crouch down and cover your head with your arms. Get underneath mattresses or heavy blankets if you can.

Definitely leave a car immediately. Try to get to a safe structure, but even being out in the open is better than a car. If you can't get to a safe structure, lie flat in a ditch or low-lying area. Cover your head with your arms. Don't get under a bridge or road overpass. As scary as tornadoes can be, if you know what to do during a twister, it can make a big difference.

MOUNTAIN WEATHER

Mountains like the Rockies have their own distinctive weather. They're usually much colder than the surrounding country. The weather there can change often, and have heavier **precipitation**.

Altitude has a huge influence on temperature. The higher you go, the colder it becomes. This is because the atmosphere acts like a blanket to keep heat in.

At higher elevations, the "blanket" isn't as thick and heat escapes. That's why many high mountains like the Rockies are always covered in snow. It never gets warm enough up there for the snow to completely melt, even in the summer.

Did You Know?

Rocky Mountain National Park in Colorado is high in elevation, so it can snow there even in July! The park frequently experiences hurricane-force winds during winter storms. One blast of wind was measured at 201 miles per hour (323 kilometers)!

If you travel west from Denver, Colorado, and drive less than an hour into the Rocky Mountains, the temperature can drop 30 degrees Fahrenheit (17 degrees Celsius) or more!

RAIN SHADOW

The western side of the Rocky Mountains receives on average more rain and snow than the east side. Why? Weather systems in the western half of the country move in from the Pacific, from west to east. As warm air passes over the Pacific Ocean, it picks up moisture. When moist air encounters mountains, the air is forced up along the slopes, where the rising air cools. Since colder air can hold less water vapor than warmer air, the water vapor in the air condenses into tiny droplets and forms clouds. Have you ever noticed clouds covering the tops of mountains? If enough water vapor condenses into droplets, it rains.

Rain Shadow

Rocky Mountains

Did You Know?

People often get weather and climate confused. Weather is what happens in the atmosphere related to temperature, precipitation, winds, and clouds. Climate is the average weather of a place over a long period of time.

As the air moves down the other side of the mountains, it warms. The air has already lost some of its moisture from raining. And now it can hold more water vapor because it is warmer. So the far side of the mountains, called a rain shadow, gets much less rainfall.

Before weather systems even get to the Rockies, the air has already lost much of its moisture as it passes over mountains along the Pacific coast. This is why even the western side of the Rockies isn't that wet. But the eastern side is even drier because it's in the rain shadow of the Rockies.

MAKE YOUR OWN
CONTINENTAL CLIMATE

1 Fill one cup about half full with sand. Fill the other cup to the same level with water. Place the thermometers upright into the water and sand. Make sure the ends of the thermometers are fully submerged.

2 Wait a few minutes, then check the temperature of the sand and water. If they aren't the same, adjust the water temperature by replacing some of the water with warmer or colder water until the temperatures are equal. Record the temperatures.

3 Place both cups on a sunny windowsill or under a strong light. Make sure the cups each receive the same amount of light, and the light doesn't hit the bulb of the thermometers directly. Record the temperatures about every 10 minutes. After about an hour, turn the light off or move the cups to the shade and let them cool. Record the temperatures about every 10 minutes.

SUPPLIES

- 2 large Styrofoam cups, the same size
- 1 cup of sand (200 grams)
- water
- 2 thermometers

What's Happening?

Land heats up and cools down faster than large bodies of water like oceans. So in the winter, air over the ocean tends to be warmer than air over land. In the summer, the reverse is true. When sea breezes move onto land in the summer, they cool the land. In the winter, they warm the land. This has the overall effect of keeping temperatures moderate for coastal areas. But land in the interior of the continent, like the Great Plains and Rocky Mountains region, has big swings between winter and summer.

MAKE YOUR OWN
TORNADO IN A BOTTLE

Washer

Oil

Water

SUPPLIES

- 2 clear, 2-liter plastic soda bottles without dents
- cold water
- a few tablespoons of vegetable oil
- small bowl
- food coloring
- 1-inch metal washer (2½ centimeters)
- duct tape
- stopwatch or clock with a second hand

1 Remove all labels, caps, and the plastic rings on the mouths of the bottles. Fill one bottle about three-quarters full with cold water.

2 Pour the oil into the small bowl and add the food coloring. Stir. Then add the mixture to the water in your bottle.

3 Place the washer on top of the bottle's mouth. Turn the second bottle upside down and place it on top of the first bottle. The mouth of the second bottle should be lined up with the washer and the mouth of the first bottle.

4 Get a friend to hold the bottles steady while you firmly wrap duct tape around the mouths of the bottles, going around several times. Press the duct tape tightly against the plastic so that it won't leak.

5 Grab the bottles where they are joined and quickly turn them upside down so that the water is in the bottle on top. Quickly swirl the bottles around a few times in circles.

6 When all the water has drained into the lower bottle, repeat step 5. This time, try timing it to see how long it takes for the water to drain. Then flip the bottles again but do not swirl the bottles around. Does the water drain faster or slower when you swirl it?

What's Happening?

Do you see a funnel in the oil and water as it flows from the top bottle into the bottom? This is like the funnel that forms in a tornado, except it's liquid. For the water to drain into the lower bottle, the air in the lower bottle has to also move into the top bottle. They have to trade places. When you swirl the water into a funnel, there's a hole in the middle so that the air can move upward at the same time the water moves downward.

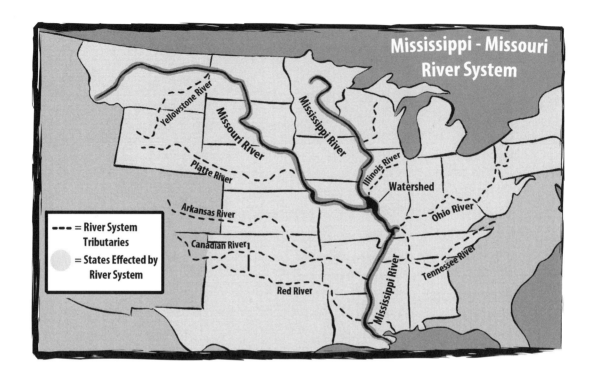

CHAPTER 6

RIVERS

The Big Muddy. The Father of Rivers. These are big names for big rivers. The Great Plains and Mountain West region contains the **headwaters** and the main section of the greatest river system in North America: the Missouri-Mississippi River system.

WORDS TO KNOW

headwater: a river's source.

tributary: a stream or river that flows into a larger river.

watershed: the land area that drains into a river or stream.

The water in rivers comes from precipitation that flows over the surface of the land. Smaller creeks and streams flow together and form bigger streams and rivers. They are called **tributaries** of the river they flow into. The land that drains into a river is the **watershed** of that river. Most rivers flow into the ocean.

HOW LONG IS IT?

When people say the Mississippi River, they usually mean the river that starts in Minnesota and ends at the Gulf of Mexico. It is 2,320 miles long (3,734 kilometers). Sometimes, especially when comparing the size of rivers in the world, people mean the Missouri River and its tributaries, as well as the Lower Mississippi River. The Missouri-Mississippi River system totals 3,745 miles long and is the third-longest river system in the world (6,027 kilometers).

The Upper Mississippi is the part of the Mississippi River from its headwaters in Minnesota to where the Ohio River joins at Cairo, Illinois. The Lower Mississippi is the part of the river from this point to the Gulf of Mexico.

Nearly all the rain that falls in the Great Plains and Mountain West region eventually drains into the Missouri and Mississippi Rivers.

MISSISSIPPI RIVER

The Mississippi River is sometimes called the Father of Rivers. This is a good nickname. It is the largest river in the United States by the amount of water it carries and the second-largest by length. Including its tributaries, the Mississippi River is the largest river system in North America. It drains 31 states from the Appalachian Mountains in the east to the Rocky Mountains in the west, and north to Canada.

If you look at a map of the Mississippi and its tributaries, it looks a bit like a tree. The trunk starts in Minnesota and ends in Louisiana at the Gulf of Mexico. Its big branches are the large rivers, or tributaries, that flow into the Mississippi. These are the Missouri and Illinois Rivers that drain into the Upper Mississippi, and the Ohio, Arkansas, and Red Rivers that drain into the Lower Mississippi.

The Mississippi starts in the cold waters of Lake Itasca in northern Minnesota. After flowing through Minnesota, it forms part of the boundary between several states, including Minnesota, Iowa, Missouri, Arkansas, and Louisiana on the west, and Wisconsin, Illinois, Kentucky, Tennessee, and Mississippi on the east.

WORDS TO KNOW

migratory bird: a bird that migrates.

confluence: the point where two or more streams flow together.

prairie: the wide, rolling land covered in grasses, west of the Mississippi River.

The Mississippi River is home to a huge variety of wildlife. There are about 240 different kinds of fish in the Mississippi, along with about 50 different mammals living in and around the river. Northern areas are home to wolves, moose, black bears, and snowy owls. The Upper Mississippi River Refuge runs for 261 miles along the river through the states of Minnesota, Wisconsin, Iowa, and Illinois (400 kilometers). It's a protected area for **migratory birds**, fish, wildlife, and plants. There are over 250 nests for bald eagles within the Refuge!

MISSOURI RIVER

The Missouri River begins in the Rocky Mountains in northwestern Montana. It's the longest river in North America, draining a watershed from 10 states.

The Missouri River begins at the **confluence** of the Gallatin, Madison, and Jefferson Rivers in Three Forks, Montana. It then flows 2,540 miles (4,088 kilometers) through canyons and **prairies** until it joins the Mississippi River just north of St. Louis, Missouri. The Yellowstone River is its largest tributary.

Numerous cities have grown up along the Missouri River. These include Bismarck in North Dakota, Pierre in South Dakota, Omaha in Nebraska, and Sioux City in Iowa. The Missouri cities of Kansas City, Jefferson City, and St. Louis are also all on the Missouri River.

WORDS TO KNOW

dam: a large, strong wall built across a river to hold back and control the water.

reservoir: an area that holds water behind a dam.

The Missouri River was called the Big Muddy in years past because it carried so much soil. One saying was that "a man jumping into the Missouri is more apt to break a leg than drown." It was a powerful river that flooded often and eroded soil. Now the river is controlled by **dams**, built to prevent flooding and provide water for crops. The water is much clearer because the sediment settles out in the **reservoirs** created by the dams.

LEWIS AND CLARK

Meriwether Lewis and William Clark were the first United States citizens to travel the entire Missouri River. The Missouri had been explored by native peoples and French explorers before, but this was the first systematic mapping of the river. Lewis and Clark started from St. Louis on May 14, 1804, where the Missouri joins the Mississippi River. They reached the source of the Missouri on July 25, 1805, at Three Forks, Montana.

OTHER RIVERS

There are many other important rivers in the middle of the country. Several drain into the Missouri and Upper Mississippi Rivers.

The Yellowstone River is the longest undammed river in the continental United States. It runs for 692 miles (1,114 kilometers), beginning near Yellowstone National Park in northwestern Wyoming. The Yellowstone flows through Montana and joins the Missouri River in North Dakota. It is known for its trout fishing.

The Illinois River flows through the state of Illinois for 273 miles (439 kilometers), joining the Mississippi River just north of St. Louis, Missouri. **Canals** connect the Illinois River to Lake Michigan, providing a link between the Great Lakes and the Gulf of Mexico. **Barges** transport goods such as grain and oil along the Illinois.

The Platte River flows for 1,026 miles before flowing into the Missouri River (1,651 kilometers). The North and South Platte Rivers both start in Colorado. The North Platte flows through Wyoming, then joins the South Platte in Nebraska to form the Platte. It drains a major portion of the central Great Plains. The Platte has been called "a mile wide and an inch deep" because it is so wide and shallow. Several hundred thousand sandhill cranes visit the Platte for four to six weeks each spring on their migration north to Canada.

Did You Know?

All up and down the Mississippi, large barges transport crops down the river. Barges are more energy efficient than trucks or even trains for transporting large loads of goods. They require less than one third as much fuel as a truck per ton of goods carried. One barge can carry 3,500 tons or more—that's as much as 134 large semi-tractor trailer trucks can carry!

STEAMBOATS

Before **steamboats**, river travel was just one-way: downriver on the current. People transported goods downriver on rafts. When they got to the end, they would take the rafts apart and sell the logs. Goods couldn't be shipped upriver. In the 1800s, steamboats were invented. A large paddle at the back of the boat was turned by a **steam engine**. These steamboats carried people and goods upriver all the way to Minnesota, and back down as well.

Many steamboats had luxurious accommodations for their wealthier passengers. There were beautiful carpets, crystal chandeliers, and fancy dinners on board.

Each steamboat had a distinctive bell that rang out at various times, including when it was time to leave **port**. The bells were often decorated. Later, steam whistles came into use as well. Boats passing each other going up and down the river had codes for which boat would go which way. Two whistle blasts meant the boat would go on the left. One whistle blast meant it would pass on the right. Many people could recognize a boat by its bell or the blast of its steam whistle.

OL' MAN RIVER

Show Boat is a famous musical about the lives of people who worked on a large Mississippi River showboat. A showboat was a barge that had plays, music, and other entertainment. *Show Boat's* most well-known song is "Ol' Man River" with the chorus:

Ol' man river, dat ol' man river
He mus' know sumpin' but don't say nuthin'
He jes' keeps rollin'
He keeps on rollin' along.

RIVER PIRATES

From the late 1700s to mid-1800s, pirates roamed the Mississippi and Ohio Rivers. They hid in caves and swamps. Pirates lured boats by calling out as if they were in trouble. The Samuel Mason Gang killed their victims, then tossed them into the Mississippi River.

If they tossed in more than one body, they would place bets on which would hit bottom first.

The Samuel Mason Gang was among the worst for about 20 years. They used Cave-in-Rock, a large cave on the Illinois side of the Ohio River, as their base. Mason was once discovered holding $7,000 and about 20 scalps!

Did You Know?

If you have a hankering for something tasty, you can try visiting these rivers.
The Blueberry River in Minnesota
The Fryingpan River in Colorado
The Apple River in Wisconsin
The Apple River in Illinois
The Artichoke River in Minnesota

FLOOD!

Rivers give life to the land, but they can also be destructive. A flood is when water covers land that is usually dry. Floods usually happen because of heavy rain or snow, when the water levels in a stream or river rise high enough to flow over its banks.

WORDS TO KNOW

floodplain: the flat land next to a river that floods when the river overflows.

levee: a wall of earth or stone built along a riverbank to prevent flooding of the land.

The Missouri and Mississippi Rivers normally overflow their banks every few years. The area that the water overflows onto is called the **floodplain** of a river. A floodplain has rich soil for farming, and provides important habitat for wildlife. But regular flooding can damage farms and houses in floodplain areas.

Beginning in the 1800s, the government began altering the flow of the Mississippi and Missouri Rivers. The U.S. Army Corps of Engineers worked to tame the river and use the energy from its flow to generate electricity. They built **levees** and dug out the channel in places to make the river deeper for boats. That was followed by the construction of dams.

MARK TWAIN

One of America's most famous writers was Mark Twain, who was a riverboat pilot as a young man. Twain was born in 1835 with the name of Samuel Clemens, but used the name Mark Twain for writing. Riverboat workers would call out "Mark Twain" when the river was a depth of two fathoms, which is about 12 feet (3½ meters). His two most famous books, *The Adventures of Tom Sawyer* and *The Adventures of Huckleberry Finn*, are set in a river town and on the Mississippi River.

But floods still occur. And although the changes to the river prevent frequent flooding, those changes can make big floods even worse. Because the river isn't allowed to overflow onto its natural floodplain, all of that extra water is kept inside the channels and the water level rises even higher.

During the Mississippi River Flood of 1927, the river overflowed its levees in 145 places in 11 states. The flooding killed 246 people and caused $400 million in damages.

From April to October 1993, the Missouri and Mississippi Rivers flooded all along their banks in nine states. Called the Great Flood of 1993, it was the worst flooding disaster since 1927. More rain and snow than normal fell from the fall of 1992 through spring 1993. It couldn't all soak into the ground so it filled the rivers. When more rain came again in the summer, the rivers flooded again and again. St. Louis had river levels 20 feet above normal (6 meters), the highest recorded in 228 years. If it had risen 2 feet higher (½ meter), it would have flooded the downtown.

Did You Know?

Levees are artificial riverbanks to prevent the river from overrunning its banks. They control the direction the river takes. Levees have been constructed along the Mississippi to provide protection from floods and keep the river in its main channel. There are more than 1,600 miles of levees along the Mississippi—that's longer than the Great Wall of China!

In all, 100,000 homes were destroyed and 50 people died. Four towns were completely destroyed. Even though the 1993 flood had only the third-largest volume of water discharge of all floods, the water level was the highest because of the levees.

The Missouri and Mississippi Floods of 2011 came less than 20 years later. During the winter and spring of 2011, record levels of rainfall and snowfall fell in the watersheds of the Missouri and Mississippi Rivers. Both the Missouri and Mississippi Rivers experienced some of the worst floods in recorded history.

The Mississippi River had risen so high that it threatened to destroy the levee system and flood towns, including Cairo, Illinois. The U.S. Army Corps of Engineers had to act quickly. For the first time in 74 years, they blasted a 2-mile-wide hole (3 kilometers) in the levee at the Birds Point-New Madrid Floodway in southeastern Missouri. This released some of the water and lowered the levels in the main river to relieve pressure on the downstream levee system. Many people were unhappy because, although it saved a number of downstream communities, it also flooded farmland.

MAKE YOUR OWN FLOOD

1 Choose a location outside to set up your experiment. It should be within reach of the water hose and in a place that is okay to get wet.

2 Set one end of the pan on top of the brick. Fill the pan with sand or soil to just below the rim. Using the spoon, scoop out a channel in the sand. It should start at the raised end, first going straight for 2 inches (5 centimeters), then bending in a stretched-out "S" shape. This is your stream channel. On one bend in the stream, build up the sand somewhat around the banks.

3 Set the hose at the top of the stream channel and turn the water on so that there is a small stream of water going into the channel. Let the water run for a few minutes.

4 Slowly increase the water flow until it begins to overflow the channel. Where does the water overflow the channel? Turn off the water and rebuild the banks in different ways. What happens if you build high banks along the upper half of the stream? What happens if you make a break in the high banks in one place?

Did You Know?

Some rivers are private and some are public. By law, rivers that are large enough to be navigated by canoe and kayak are owned by the public (that includes you) up to the high water mark.

What's Happening?

Engineers have built up levees along parts of the Missouri and Mississippi Rivers. This has changed how often and where floods occur, just like in your stream channel.

CHAPTER 7

ECOSYSTEMS

Imagine looking out over a vast expanse of tall grass, gently waving in the wind. It ripples with different colors—browns, greens, yellows, and even reds. Then imagine walking through grass with stems higher than your head. If you were an early settler in this country heading west, this is what you would have encountered as you entered the prairie.

From afar, the prairie looks like a simple, flat, green area. But up close, it's clear the prairie is an amazing ecosystem. An ecosystem is all the plants and animals that live in a place. It's also the physical environment itself—the soil, air, water, and even the sunlight.

Everything in an ecosystem interacts with each other. The plants need the soil and sunlight of a certain place, the animals eat the plants, and the plants depend on the animals.

PRAIRIE: A SEA OF GRASS

Prairies are grasslands that extend for many miles. When European settlers first saw the prairie they called it a sea of grass. Hundreds of different types of grass can grow in grasslands, along with many types of flowering plants, called forbs. There are very few trees or shrubs.

Grasslands often grow in the middle of continents. These areas don't receive enough rain to grow a forest, but get too much rain to be a desert. Prairies are hot in the summer and cold in the winter. They are often windy. In the United States, the original prairie stretched throughout all of the Great Plains. Most of that prairie has been converted to farmland because the soil is very **fertile**, but there are patches of prairie still left here and there.

WORDS TO KNOW

fertile: land that is good for growing plants.

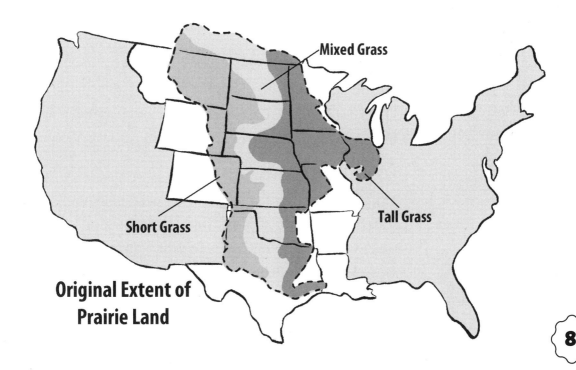

Mixed Grass

Short Grass

Tall Grass

Original Extent of Prairie Land

There are three types of prairie in the United States.

Tall grass prairie is found in the eastern portion of the prairie, where it receives 25 to 39 inches of rain per year (63 to 74 centimeters). The grass grows tall—up to 6 feet tall, and occasionally even 10 feet tall (2–3 meters)! Some of the most common tall grasses are Indian grass, big bluestem, little bluestem, and switchgrass.

Short grass prairie is in the western area of the prairie, a 200-mile swath (322 kilometers) running along the eastern foothills of the Rocky Mountains. This area receives less than 10 inches of rainfall per year (25 centimeters). The grasses here grow up to about 12 inches tall (30 centimeters) and include blue grama and buffalograss.

Mixed-grass prairie is the area between the tall grass and short grass sections. It receives 14 to 23 inches of rain per year (35 to 59 centimeters). A mixture of short and tall grasses grow here.

Did You Know?

Grasslands are known by many different names: Prairies in North America, pampas in South America, steppes in Eurasia, veld in South Africa, and bush or downs in Australia. Savannas are grasslands that receive somewhat more rain and have trees scattered throughout.

Prairies have numerous grazing animals, burrowing animals, birds, and lots and lots of insects. Predators can include wolves, badgers, hawks, owls, and coyotes. What are some plants and animals that make prairies unique?

GRASS

Grasses have thin, hollow stems and straight, narrow leaves. The flowers are feathery at the top of the stem, without petals. Grasses grow from their base. So when animals eat the grass, it grows back. Grasses can reproduce by seeds as well as by sending out long underground stems.

Prairie grasses aren't like your grass at home, which is probably just one type of grass. The prairie has many types of grasses all growing together. They have interesting names like devil's darning needle, squirreltail, puffsheath dropseed, and weeping love grass.

Prairie grasses have deep roots—as deep as 6 feet (2 meters). In fact, up to 75 percent of the plant mass in prairies is below ground. This allows them to reach water even when there's little rain. It also allows them to easily regrow after fires. Trees and shrubs are killed in fires and take much longer to reseed and grow.

It might seem the opposite of what you'd expect, but prairie grasses actually need fires to compete against other types of plants and survive.

Sod

Grass: Puffsheath Grass   **Forbs: Purple Cone Flower**

Sod is a layer of dead grass and the roots of the plants, all tangled up together. Early settlers on the prairie built houses out of sod because there were no trees around for wood. The walls could be 2 feet thick (½ meter)! Sod houses kept people warm, but it was hard to keep out insects. After a good rainstorm the roof could drip for days.

WORDS TO KNOW

graze: to eat grass.
regurgitate: to bring food up from the stomach to the mouth.

Did You Know?

Grass can't be eaten by most animals because it is hard to digest. **Grazing** animals, such as bison and elk, have special stomachs to help them slowly digest the grass. They **regurgitate** the partially digested grass, called cud. They chew the cud, and swallow it again.

FORBS

Forbs are flowering plants. Some of the forbs you might find in prairies are purple coneflower, leadplant, compass plant, and rattlesnake plant. Many animals depend on particular types of forbs. For example, the monarch butterfly needs the milkweed plant to lay its eggs, and the regal fritillary butterfly feeds on violets.

Did You Know?

Pocket gophers, which are related to prairie dogs, can burrow up to 300 feet in one night (91 meters). Their lips close behind their teeth so they don't get dirt in their mouths.

PRAIRIE DOGS

Prairie dogs aren't dogs at all. They are a type of ground squirrel with a head and body about a foot long and a tail a few inches long (30 centimeters and 10 centimeters). You'll see them sitting up on their hind legs with their front paws folded on their stomachs. Like other rodents, their teeth keep growing.

Why don't you see prairie dogs with giant teeth? They wear them down by gnawing and chewing.

Prairie dogs are social animals. Groups of prairie dogs build huge underground burrows. A collection of burrows is called a town. They greet members in their group by a touching of noses that looks like kissing! But they chase away prairie dogs from other towns.

Prairie dog towns can cover many acres and go as deep as 15 feet (4½ meters)! There are winding tunnels connecting various rooms, with "bathrooms" for their droppings, grass-lined "bedrooms" where they sleep, and "kitchens" where they store food. The opening to a burrow is mounded up so water can't enter during floods. There's usually a prairie dog sitting by the mound as a lookout for predators. If he sees a predator, he calls out "Yip! Yip! Yip!" and does a back flip to warn others to dive underground.

Did You Know?

The largest prairie dog town ever found contained about 400 million animals. It was in Texas and was about 100 miles wide and 250 miles long (161 by 402 kilometers). That's larger than 10 states!

Prairie dog towns have often been destroyed because prairie dogs dig up crops. But they also mix up the soil and their tunnels provide homes for other animals such as burrowing owls. Prairie dogs are an important source of food for black-footed ferrets, hawks, and coyotes. Many people are now trying to restore areas for prairie dogs to burrow.

LOCUSTS

You can find lots of insects on the prairie, munching on its delicious grass. One of the most common is the grasshopper, which can jump 20 times the length of its body. If you could jump like a grasshopper, you would be able to jump nearly 100 feet (30 meters)!

WORDS TO KNOW

swarm: a large number of insects flying together.

locusts: another name for grasshoppers when they swarm.

hide: the skin of an animal.

drought: a long period of time without rain.

extinct: when a group of plants or animals dies out and there are no more left in the world.

Grasshoppers bunch together in huge numbers when there isn't rain for a long time. When they **swarm**, they're called **locusts**. A swarm can rise as high as a mile (1½ kilometers)! Then the locusts swoop down and devour any plants around. There can be billions of locusts in a swarm and it can look like a black cloud. In 1870 there was a swarm in Nebraska that was estimated to contain 124 billion locusts. It was 100 miles long and 1 mile high (161 kilometers long and 1½ kilometers high). The swarm took six hours to pass.

BISON

Bison, sometimes called American buffalo, are amazing, massive creatures. They are about 6 feet high at the shoulder (12 meters), and weigh as much as a small car! They have a huge, woolly head and hump, and large, curved horns. Their bellowing call sounds like a cross between a lion's roar and thunder. Bison usually run in herds of 50 to 200.

There used to be as many as 75 million bison roaming the prairies. Native Americans had always hunted bison for food and their **hides**. By the mid-1800s, Europeans and Native Americans hunted the bison using horses and firearms, greatly increasing the number of bison killed each year. Even more bison died because of **drought**. Such huge numbers of bison died in the 1800s that they nearly became **extinct**.

Bison

Because of protections put in place there are now about 30,000 wild bison and about 500,000 more that are raised for their meat and hides. You might encounter wild bison at Yellowstone National Park in Wyoming and Wind Cave National Park in South Dakota.

Did You Know?

In Yellowstone National Park, more people are injured by bison than by bears. Bison will sometimes attack humans if they are provoked. Even though they look slow, they can run up to 35 miles per hour (56 kilometers)!

WHERE HAVE ALL THE PRAIRIES GONE?

The tallgrass prairie used to cover a huge area, from North Dakota to Ohio and Minnesota to Texas. Elk, deer, bison, and pronghorn thrived, with wolves, grizzly bears, and coyotes hunting them. Today, most of that prairie is gone. More than 96 percent has been turned into farmland. What's left is just small patches in places where it's hard to farm. But there aren't any large areas of prairie that support the variety of wildlife that used to live there. There are just a few places where the prairie has been left intact or where people are trying to rebuild it.

• Flint Hills National Wildlife Refuge in Kansas has 18,500 acres of prairie. Ducks and geese use the Refuge during their spring and fall migrations.

• The Neal Smith National Wildlife Refuge southwest of Prairie City, Iowa, was purchased in 1989 when it was just a huge area of cornfields. Scientists are using seeds and fire to restore 4,000 acres of prairie. They have had to find the right variety of seeds for the restored prairie. First they intentionally set fires to clear space for prairie grasses to grow. Their efforts have successfully restored a thriving prairie. One scientist in the Refuge found 30 different kinds of insects in different stages of life on one single plant! The regal fritillary butterfly is now living in the Neal Smith National Wildlife Refuge. The regal fritillary is a large, orange, butterfly that hadn't been seen in that part of Iowa for more than 100 years.

• Tallgrass Prairie Preserve in Oklahoma has 39,000 acres of preserved tallgrass prairie, the largest preserved tract of native tallgrass prairie in the world. There are over 700 species of plants, 300 bird species, and 80 mammal species on the preserve. About 2,500 bison roam much of the area.

PRONGHORN

Pronghorn are grazing animals related to antelope. They are a little over 3 feet tall at the shoulder (1 meter) and have two branched horns. They are special because they can sprint as fast as 53 miles per hour (85 kilometers an hour), which is almost as fast as a car on the highway. Pronghorn are the fastest animal in North America and one of the fastest in the world. They have long legs and an extra large heart that helps them pump oxygen when they run.

Pronghorn

DIRT: YOUR LIFE DEPENDS ON IT

Step onto some grass. Beneath the grass is dirt, which scientists call **soil**. Without soil, we wouldn't have all of the fruits and vegetable we like to eat, or any of the animals that eat those plants. Soil on prairies is deep, dark, and fertile, with lots of **organic material**, which means it is good for feeding plants. Prairie soil has formed over thousands of years. It is so good that people have taken over nearly all of the areas once covered by prairies for farms. And the farms on the Great Plains are some of the most productive farms in the world.

WORDS TO KNOW

soil: the top layer of the earth, including tiny rock particles mixed with organic material.

organic material: decomposed plant and animal material.

Plants such as wheat and corn don't have deep roots. This means they don't hold the soil in place as well as prairie grasses. In the 1930s, during several years of drought, the soil dried out. Wind picked up the loose soil and blew it for hundreds of miles in huge clouds. Soil sometimes covered half a house overnight and formed drifts up to 25 feet high (7½ meters)! In 1936, the Soil Conservation Service was formed to help people develop better ways of farming to prevent soil erosion.

MAKE YOUR OWN
HOOP COUNTS

1 Find a field or meadow. If you can, pick a place that hasn't been used to grow crops in awhile. The plants should be growing naturally.

2 Toss the hula hoop onto the ground. Now count the number of plant species that are inside the hula hoop. In your notebook, write a brief description of each type of plant, including grasses, shrubs, and flowering plants.

3 Do the same thing in two or three other places in the field.

4 Now record the number of species inside your hula hoop in a few places on your lawn, or on the grass in a park. Which place has more plant species?

SUPPLIES

- hula hoop
- notebook
- pencil
- magnifying glass

What's Happening?

Grass lawns are great places for running and playing, but they're not the best places for plant **diversity**. They are what is called a monoculture, where just one type of plant is grown. Prairies have many, many types of plants to help them resist damage from diseases and insects. With a variety of plants, they also form habitats for many different types of animals.

WORDS TO KNOW

diversity: when many different people or things exist within a group or place.

MAKE YOUR OWN
GRASSY "TREE"

1 Line the shoebox lid with wax paper. Fill the lid with the soil and sprinkle grass seed on top. Lightly spray the mixture with water using the spray bottle. Make sure the spray bottle you use is either new or has only held water.

2 Hold the pine cones under running water for a minute to get them completely wet.

3 Set the pine cones upright in the soil in the shoebox lid. Gently press some soil onto the tops of the pine cones and the scales of each pine cone. Press the grass seed into the soil. Spray all of the soil until it's moist.

SUPPLIES

- lid of a shoebox
- wax paper
- potting soil
- grass seed
- water
- spray bottle
- one or more pine cones

4 Place the shoebox lid on a sunny windowsill. Over the next few days, lightly spray the soil in the lid and on the pine cones to keep everything moist. You'll need to spray the soil several times a day. Use scissors to give your grass a haircut if it needs it.

5 If you'd like, you can try different types of grass seed on different pine cones. Notice the differences in what they look like and how long they take to **germinate**.

WORDS TO KNOW

germinate: to start growing from seed.

What's Happening?

Grass seed germinates fairly easily. All it needs is moisture, warmth, and some soil. Once they start, the tiny grass plants need light to be able to make their own food and grow. If your grass seed didn't germinate, the most likely reason is that it dried out. Try again and keep the soil moist.

GROW YOUR OWN
SUNFLOWERS

1 Fill the pot with the potting soil. Add water to the soil until it is damp, but not soaked.

2 Plant 2 or 3 sunflower seeds in the pot. Cover the seeds with as much soil as is indicated on the seed package. Gently water the seeds and place the pot on a sunny windowsill.

3 When the sunflower plants are a few inches high (about 8 centimeters), notice which one is the biggest and healthiest. Pull out all the others, leaving the biggest one to continue growing.

SUPPLIES

- pot with a drainage hole in the bottom
- potting soil
- water
- package of sunflower seeds

4 Once the danger of frost is gone where you live, you can transplant your sunflower outside. Choose a sunny place that isn't windy.

5 Dig a hole that is bigger than your pot. Carefully lift your soil and plant out of the pot and place it in the hole. Water your plant and place a wooden stake behind it. When the plant grows larger, tie the plant to the stake so it won't droop over.

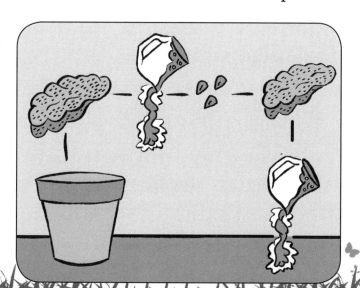

6 You can also plant sunflower seeds directly in the ground. You'll have to wait a bit longer to start so you can plant the seeds after the danger of frost is gone. Plant an entire row of sunflowers along a fence. Or create a square shape to form a sunflower house.

What's Happening?

Sunflowers are one of many types of flowers that are native to the prairie. The sunflower is the state flower of Kansas and a symbol of the prairie. This is a fun project to start in early spring.

CHAPTER 8

THE GREAT LAKES

If you stand on the shores of Lake Superior, you might think that you're standing on the shores of an ocean. The water spreads out as far as you can see. The waves can be huge. And the beaches are like those on the Atlantic or Pacific Oceans.

But take a swim in the water and you'll soon realize there's one big difference: the water of Lake Superior—and all of the Great Lakes—doesn't taste salty. These are freshwater lakes. The Great Lakes support human communities large and small, and a huge variety of plants and animals.

The Great Lakes are made up of five lakes. Lake Superior is the largest lake, and the highest in elevation. Water flows from Lake Superior down the St. Marys River for 60 miles (97 kilometers) to Lake Huron. Lake Michigan is connected to Lake Huron by the deep Straits of Mackinac. From a water point of view, Michigan and Huron are considered to be one lake, because the levels of the lakes rise and fall together.

Did You Know?

Even though each lake has its own separate basin, all of the lakes are connected. They're also connected to the Atlantic Ocean.

Water then flows from Lake Huron down the St. Clair River, through Lake St. Clair, and down the Detroit River to reach Lake Erie. From Lake Erie, water travels down the Niagara River, over the Niagara Falls, and into Lake Ontario. The man-made Welland Canal goes around Niagara Falls to allow ships to pass. Finally, water flows from Lake Ontario into the St. Lawrence River and the Atlantic Ocean.

The Great Lakes & Waterways

GREAT LAKES QUICK FACTS

- The Great Lakes hold 21 percent of the freshwater on Earth and are the largest group of freshwater lakes by surface area in the world. That means that for every 5 gallons of freshwater in the world (19 liters), 1 gallon of it is in the Great Lakes (3¾ liters).

- The Great Lakes hold enough water to cover the entire continental United States in 9½ feet of water (3 meters)!

- The Great Lakes border seven states: Michigan, Wisconsin, Minnesota, Illinois, Ohio, Pennsylvania, and New York.

- Lake Superior is the largest, deepest, coldest, and cleanest of the lakes. It is 1,332 feet deep (406 meters), and holds one-tenth of the world's freshwater. By surface area, it is the largest lake in the world. The average water temperature is 40 degrees Fahrenheit (4 degrees Celsius). Brrrr!

- Lake Erie is only 210 feet deep at its deepest (64 meters), and it freezes over quickly in the winter.

- Lake Michigan is the only lake that is completely within the United States borders. The other four border both the United States and Canada.

- There are over 35,000 islands in all of the Great Lakes.

- The Great Lakes take up as much space as New York, New Jersey, Connecticut, Rhode Island, Massachusetts, Vermont, and New Hampshire combined.

- Lake Michigan splits the state of Michigan into two parts called the Upper Peninsula and the Lower Peninsula.

HOW THEY WERE FORMED

The Great Lakes are both old and young. Their roots are deep—they got their start over one billion years ago. That's when the North American continent began rifting apart. If it had kept going, a new ocean would have formed. The rifting stopped, but it left an arch-shaped basin. The top of the arch is where Lake Superior is now, and its north shore is the northern arc of the rift. Another rift started 570 million years ago that formed the basins for the St. Lawrence River and Lakes Ontario and Erie. These two rifts shaped the land into broad basins, but the land was still dry at this point.

About 10,000 years ago, during the last ice age, the region was covered by glaciers more than a mile thick (1.6 kilometers).

The glaciers pressed down on the land and carved out depressions and valleys. When the earth warmed and the glaciers melted, the water filled the valleys to form the Great Lakes.

WORDS TO KNOW

mollusk: an animal with a soft body protected by a shell, such as a clam or snail.

sand dune: a hill of sand.

SHORELINE

Beaches, marshes, bogs, sand dunes, and rocky shores are all found at the Great Lakes. The shorelines are diverse because of the variety of underlying rocks, the changing climate, and the carving by glaciers.

Sandy beaches are the most common type of shoreline. You can find migratory shorebirds, insects, and **mollusks** here. And of course humans! The **sand dunes** of the Great Lakes are the largest freshwater coastal dunes in the world. The most famous are the Sleeping Bear Dunes on Lake Michigan. The dunes there can reach as high as 400 feet (122 meters) along the beaches.

WORDS TO KNOW

wetland: an area located around lakes and rivers that contains a lot of soil moisture.

fishery: a place for catching fish.

overfishing: when so many fish are caught each year that there are not enough left.

parasite: a living thing that feeds off another living thing.

Wetlands, such as marshes, swamps, and bogs, may not sound like a fun place to go. But wetlands support an incredible variety of life. They are the most productive ecosystems in the world. Any area that is not dry land, but isn't open water either, is a wetland. Migratory birds love wetlands, where they can feast on insects and mollusks.

POLLUTION

In June 1969, the Cuyahoga River, which flows into Lake Erie, caught fire as it flowed through Cleveland, Ohio. People were horrified. How could a river catch fire? It was so polluted with oil and chemicals floating on top, creating a brown, oily sheen, that it burned.

For many years, people had dumped chemicals, raw sewage, and even dead animals in the Cuyahoga and other rivers feeding the Great Lakes.

FISHING

The Great Lakes are one of the largest **fisheries** in the world. Some of the most common species caught include whitefish, trout, salmon, walleye, and perch. Lake Erie is the most productive fishery of the Great Lakes. The largest catches recorded were in 1888 and 1899 at 147 million pounds of fish (67 million kilograms)!

Pollution and **overfishing** have reduced the amount of fish caught since then. But fish numbers are increasing as people work to protect the lakes. Each year, the Great Lakes fishery is worth more than four billion dollars.

People thought the water would take care of the waste. The problems began in the 1700s with overfishing and the damming up of rivers. Later, fertilizer used by farmers and homeowners was washed into the lakes. Algae, which love fertilizer, grew rapidly. But algae used up all of the oxygen in the lakes, and there wasn't enough for fish.

By the 1960s, Lake Erie was covered in algae slime and declared "Dead."

The burning Cuyahoga River was a wake-up call, and people started cleaning up the rivers and lakes. New laws, including the Clean Water Act and agreements between the United States and Canada, have helped to restore the Great Lakes. There's still more work to do, but the lakes are no longer dead. The fish are returning to the Cuyahoga River.

VAMPIRES!

In the 1930s, a kind of "vampire" entered the Great Lakes. This vampire doesn't wear a black cape, and doesn't have fangs, but it does suck blood. Fish blood, that is. It's called a sea lamprey. Sea lampreys have a snakelike body and are **parasites** to many fish. They don't have jaws, but they attach onto fish with their mouths and suck their blood. By the 1950s, lampreys had almost wiped out many fish. Lakes Michigan and Huron lost almost their entire trout populations.

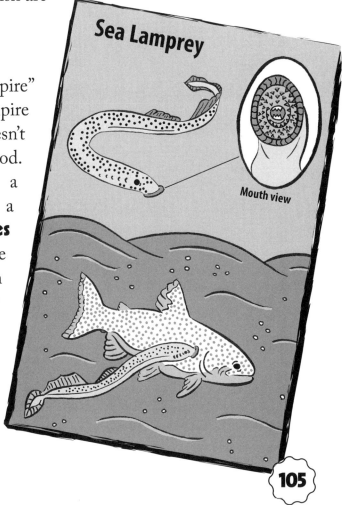

Sea Lamprey

Mouth view

WORDS TO KNOW

invasive species: a species that is not native to an ecosystem and that is harmful to the ecosystem in some way.

native species: a species that is native to an ecosystem.

ballast: fresh or salt water carried by ships to help balance the ship.

suspension bridge: a bridge whose road is suspended from two or more cables that pass over towers.

Invasive species are plants or animals that come into an area from elsewhere and have a negative impact on the ecosystem. Lampreys are among the worst of invasive species, but they're not the only ones. Many invasive species compete for space or food, crowding out **native species**.

There have been over 160 species of plants and animals introduced into the Great Lakes in the last century or so. Most came in as "passengers" on ships. Ships carry **ballast** to help balance the ship. Ballast is picked up and discharged in ports, and plants and animals can be accidentally taken on in one place, then let go in another.

Other invasive species include:

- Purple loosestrife, which has displaced native plants along the lake shores.

- Goby, a fish that lives on the lake bottom and eats tremendous amounts of food.

- Zebra mussels, which are fingernail-sized mussels with a striped pattern on their shells. They were first discovered in the Great Lakes in the 1960s and in 10 years had spread throughout all of the lakes. These mussels have now been found all the way down the Mississippi River. Zebra mussels clog pipes and encrust any hard surface, including ship bottoms and even other mussels.

Did You Know?

The Mackinac Bridge (called "Big Mac") is the world's third-longest **suspension bridge**. It's about 5 miles long (8 kilometers) and crosses the Straits of Mackinac where Lakes Michigan and Huron meet.

LAKES AND ISLANDS

Manitoulin Island on Lake Huron is the largest island in any inland body of water in the world. Isle Royale in Lake Superior is the second-largest island. And both of these islands have lakes within them. Within Manitoulin Island, Lake Manitou is the largest lake located on a freshwater island in the world. You can call it a "lake in a lake." And guess what? Lake Manitou has small islands. So those islands are islands in a lake on an island in a lake!

A potential invasive species that has people worried is the Asian Carp. This fish can weigh up to 100 pounds (45 kilograms), grow 4 feet long (1¼ meters), and live for 25 years. Asian Carp are established in the Mississippi River and have been slowly migrating north.

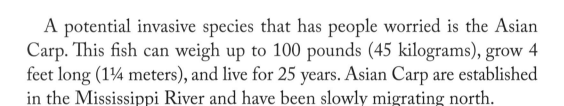

Because they are so big, these carp consume much of the food resources of other fish.

The Great Lakes are connected to the Mississippi River by a man-made canal, named the Chicago Sanitary and Ship Canal. It allows goods and people to move between the Great Lakes and the Mississippi River. But that connection also allows unwanted species to migrate between the lakes and the river as well.

Asian Carp

For now, a series of three electric barriers keep the fish out of the Great Lakes. But many people are concerned that the fish could get through those barriers. Some people, especially those in the fishing industry, want to close the Chicago Sanitary and Ship Canal. This would keep the carp out. But others, especially in the shipping industry, favor keeping the canal open.

SHIPPING

The Great Lakes are an important place for shipping goods around the central United States. There are 63 commercial ports on the lakes, and over 150 million tons of **cargo** is shipped in a year (136 million metric tons). Most shipping on the Great Lakes is in **raw materials** such as iron ore, limestone, grain, and coal.

LAKES SLANG

The Great Lakes have some of their own slang terms:

Third Coast: the shores of the Great Lakes, especially Lake Michigan.

Boat: term for any ship, no matter how big it is.

Laker: a boat that trades on the lakes.

Salties: ocean-going boats temporarily in the Great Lakes.

WORDS TO KNOW

icebreaker: a ship built for breaking a passage through frozen water.

Freighters that carry these raw materials can travel between all of the lakes and out to the ocean. The automotive industry, centered in Detroit on Lake Michigan, is located in the Great Lakes region because the lakes make it easy to transport materials.

The lakes freeze over in many areas in winter. Ships called **icebreakers** keep the shipping lanes open in winter. Icebreakers are specially designed to be able to break through ice-covered water. They have powerful engines that push the bow, or front of the ship, up onto the ice. Then the weight of the ship breaks the ice. An icebreaker has a special shape that pushes the broken ice out of the way. They are also especially strong to withstand the battering they take.

Did You Know?

The Witch Tree (also called Little Spirit Cedar Tree) in Grand Portage, Minnesota, is a tree that has clung to boulders at the edge of Lake Superior for at least 300 years. It's gnarled and stunted. You would be too if you were living on a rock and battered by storm waves! This tree is considered sacred by the Ojibwa Indians.

MAKE YOUR OWN
TEMPERATURE GRADIENTS

1 Rinse out all of the containers and remove any labels. Fill the large bucket with tap water.

2 Place the bowl inside the bucket and turn it upside down so that no air remains in the bowl. Set it on the bottom of the bucket.

3 Fill one bottle with ice water (but don't put ice in the bottle). Add a few drops of one color of food coloring. Fill the other bottle with hot tap water and add a few drops of the other color of food coloring. Place the bottle caps back on each bottle and gently tighten the caps.

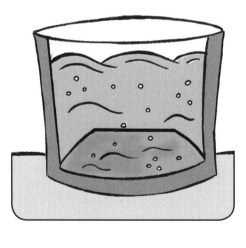

110

4 Place each bottle on its side on top of the bowl inside the bucket. Remove both bottle caps. Watch what happens to the ice water! What happens to the hot water?

What's Happening?

The water separates into layers because of differences in the density of the water. Hotter water is less dense and colder water is more dense. The denser, colder water sinks to the bottom, and the less dense, warmer water rises to the top.

The same thing happens in the Great Lakes. There are layers of temperature, with warmer temperatures near the surface. The water becomes colder with depth. In some places, the water changes as much as 26 degrees Fahrenheit in just 10 feet (3 meters)! The water at the bottom of the lakes is close to freezing.

Upwelling is when colder water rises to the surface because of winds moving the surface water. These colder waters often bring nutrients up and create abundant fisheries.

MAKE YOUR OWN
SAND DUNES

1 Make a cardboard tray to hold the sand: Select the side of the box that has the longest length and width. Set that side on the floor. Cut the cardboard box so that it is open on the top and has a 6-inch-high wall (15 centimeters).

2 Scoop sand into the cardboard tray so the sand is a few inches deep (about 8 centimeters).

3 Using the blow dryer, blow sand so that it piles up into dune shapes. DO THIS OUTDOORS!

4 Try placing different size rocks in the box, and blow towards the rocks. Can you make the dunes different shapes by changing wind directions? What happens when you sprinkle water on the sand? Try blowing the sand into a small dune, then sprinkle some water directly on the dune and blow dry sand on top of that. Is it easier or harder to make taller dunes? What happens if all of the sand is wet?

What's Happening?

The Great Lakes are known for their sandy beaches and sand dunes. How do sand dunes form? You need two things in addition to sand: wind that's strong, steady, and that sometimes reverses directions, and conditions that keep the sand loose. Varying these components makes different-shaped dunes. In addition, vegetation sorts and traps the sand. Sand dunes have formed along the coasts of all of the Great Lakes. The best-known of these dunes are along the coasts of Lake Michigan, which contains the largest concentration of fresh water dunes in the world!

The dunes along Lake Michigan formed thousands of years ago when glaciers covered the land. The glaciers transported large amounts of sand to the area. When the glaciers finally retreated about 3,000 years ago, they dumped out the sand as the ice melted. Then the wind and water formed the sand into dunes. That process continues today, as waves cut away the bases of bluffs, and wind blows the sand upward to be deposited on top of the dunes. Vegetation like grasses and shrubs traps the sand and holds it in place.

The Great Lakes have a great variety of sand dune types. Parabolic dunes are crescent-shaped dunes that are anchored by plants. Perched dunes have formed on top of glacial moraines. Linear dunes are long dunes that form parallel to the shoreline. And transverse dunes form perpendicular to the wind.

acidic: from acids, which are chemical compounds that taste sour.

adapt: changes a plant or animal makes to survive.

alpine glacier: a glacier that forms in the mountains.

altitude: the height above sea level. Also called elevation.

Ancestral Rockies: a mountain chain that formed over 300 million years ago. These mountains were eroded, but the rocks formed then can be seen in today's Rocky Mountains.

asthenosphere: the semi-molten middle layer of the earth that includes the lower mantle. Much of the asthenosphere flows slowly, like Silly Putty.

atmosphere: the air surrounding the earth.

atom: the smallest particle of matter that cannot be broken down without changing the particle's properties. Everything on Earth is made of various combinations of atoms.

ballast: fresh or salt water carried by ships to help balance the ship.

barge: a boat with a flat bottom used to carry loads on canals and rivers.

basin: a low area shaped like a bowl.

bird of prey: a bird that hunts animals for food.

blizzard: a severe snow storm with high winds, low temperatures, and heavy snow.

brittle: describes a solid that breaks when put under pressure. A blade of grass will bend, but a dry twig is brittle and will break.

caldera: a large volcanic crater, usually formed by a large eruption that collapsed the mouth of the volcano.

canal: a man-made waterway.

carbon dioxide: a gas formed by the rotting of plants and animals and when animals breathe out.

carbonic acid: a weak acid formed when carbon dioxide dissolves in water.

cargo: goods carried by ship.

cave: a natural underground opening connected to the surface, large enough for a person to enter.

cavern: a very large cave or system of connected caves.

cirque: a basin at the head of a glacial valley, which often contains a lake.

climate: the average weather of an area over a long period of time.

condense: to change from a gas to a liquid.

confluence: the point where two or more streams flow together.

continental: relating to the earth's large land masses.

continental climate: the climate found in the middle of a continent. It is characterized by large variations in temperature and four seasons.

continental platform: the central, stable part of the craton that is covered by sediments and sedimentary rocks.

continental shield: the part of the craton where the ancient rocks are exposed and are not covered by sediments.

convergent boundary: where two plates come together.

core: the center of the earth, composed of the metals iron and nickel. The core has two parts—a solid inner core, and a liquid outer core.

craton: the stable, central part of a continent.

crust: the thick, outer layer of the earth.

current: a constantly moving mass of liquid.

dam: a large, strong wall built across a river to hold back and control the water.

dense: tightly packed.

divergent boundary: where two plates are moving in opposite directions, sometimes called a rift zone. New crust forms at rift zones from the magma pushing through the crust.

diversity: when many different people or things exist within a group or place.

drought: a long period of time without rain.

earthquake: a sudden movement in the outer layer of the earth. It releases stress built up from the motion of the earth's plates.

ecosystem: a community of plants and animals living in the same area and relying on each other to survive.

element: a substance that is made up of atoms that are all the same.

Enhanced Fujita scale: a scale used to measure the strength of tornadoes based on the destruction they cause. The scale runs from EF-0 to EF-5, with EF-5 being the strongest.

epicenter: the point on the earth's surface directly above the location of the earthquake.

erosion: the wearing away and carrying off of materials on the earth's surface.

erupt: to burst out suddenly.

extinct: when a group of plants or animals dies out and there are no more left in the world.

fault: a crack in the outer layer of the earth.

fertile: land that is good for growing plants.

firn: granular snow that has not yet been compressed into ice.

fishery: a place for catching fish.

floodplain: the flat land next to a river that floods when the river overflows.

freshwater: water that is not salty.

fumarole: a vent that lets out hot gases.

geography: the study of the earth and its features, especially the shape of the land, and the effect of human activity.

geologist: a scientist who studies the earth and its movements.

geology: the scientific study of the history and physical nature of the earth.

germinate: to start growing from seed.

geyser: a hot spring that periodically ejects water and steam in the air.

glacial period: a period of time within an ice age when a large part of the earth's surface is covered with ice.

glacier: a huge mass of ice and snow.

granule: a small grain or pellet.

grassland: a large area of land covered with grass.

gravity: the force that pulls objects to the earth.

graze: to eat grass.

habitat: the natural area where a plant or animal lives.

hail: balls of ice and frozen snow that fall like rain.

half-life: the amount of time it takes for one half of a radioactive parent element to decay to its daughter.

hanging valley: a side valley that joins the main valley at a higher level. It forms when a smaller glacier doesn't erode as deeply as the main glacier.

headwater: a river's source.

hide: the skin of an animal.

hotspot: an area in the middle of a plate, where hot magma rises to the surface.

hot spring: a natural pool of water that is heated by hot or molten rock. Hot springs are found in areas of volcanic activity.

hydrosphere: the earth's water, including oceans, rivers, lakes, glaciers, and water vapor in the air.

Ice Age: a period of time when large ice sheets cover large areas of land. It particularly refers to the most recent series of glaciations during the Pleistocene. An ice age can include shorter periods when glaciers retreat, as well as periods when the glaciers grow.

icebreaker: a ship built for breaking a passage through frozen water.

igneous rock: rock that forms from cooling magma.

interglacial period: a period within an ice age that is somewhat warmer and glaciers retreat.

invasive species: a species that is not native to an ecosystem and that is harmful to the ecosystem in some way.

jet stream: a high-speed flow of air high in the atmosphere that flows from west to east and often brings weather with it.

levee: a wall of earth or stone built along a riverbank to prevent flooding of the land.

limestone: a sedimentary rock that forms from the skeletons and shells of sea creatures. Limestone erodes easily.

lithosphere: the rigid outer layer of the earth that includes the crust and the upper mantle.

lobe: an extension of a glacier, with a shape like a tongue. The Wisconsin glaciation had six major lobes.

locusts: another name for grasshoppers when they swarm.

magma: partially melted rock below the surface of the earth.

mantle: the middle layer of the earth. The upper mantle, together with the crust, forms the lithosphere.

metamorphic rock: rock that has been transformed by heat or pressure or both into new rock, while staying solid.

meteorologist: a scientist who studies and forecasts climate and weather.

migrate: to move from one place to another each year.

migratory bird: a bird that migrates.

mollusk: an animal with a soft body protected by a shell, such as a clam or snail.

molten: melted by heat to form a liquid.

moraine: an accumulation of gravel and sand deposited at the front of a glacier.

mud pot: a boiling area of mud.

native species: a species that is native to an ecosystem.

oceanic: in or from the ocean.

organic material: decomposed plant and animal material.

overfishing: when so many fish are caught each year that there are not enough left.

parasite: a living thing that feeds off another living thing.

plains: a flat expanse of land.

plateau: a large, raised area that is fairly flat.

plates: huge, moving, interconnected slabs of lithosphere.

plate tectonics: the theory that describes how plates move across the earth and interact with each other to produce earthquakes, volcanoes, and mountains.

Pleistocene: the epoch in geologic history from about 2.5 million years ago to 10,000 years ago that experienced repeated glaciations.

port: a place where ships can load and unload.

prairie: the wide, rolling land covered in grasses, west of the Mississippi River.

precipitation: the falling to earth of rain, snow, or any form of water.

predator: an animal that hunts another animal for food.

radiometric dating: a method of determining the age of rocks. It looks at a radioactive element in rock, such as uranium, and measures how much it has decayed.

raw material: a resource used in factories to make things.

regurgitate: to bring food up from the stomach to the mouth.

reservoir: an area that holds water behind a dam.

Richter scale: a scale used to measure the strength of an earthquake.

rifting: when the lithosphere splits apart.

rock flour: fine-grained sediment made from glaciers grinding over bedrock.

Rocky Mountains: a mountain range running from New Mexico into Canada.

sand dune: a hill of sand.

sediment: loose rock particles such as sand or clay.

sedimentary rock: rock formed from the compression of sediments, the remains of plants and animals, or from the evaporation of seawater.

seismic wave: a wave of energy generated from an earthquake. The wave travels through the earth.

seismograph: an instrument that measures the intensity of a seismic wave.

soil: the top layer of the earth, including tiny rock particles mixed with organic material.

species: a group of plants or animals that are related and look the same.

speleothem: a distinctive cave formation, such as a stalactite.

stalactite: a cave formation that looks like an icicle hanging from the ceiling.

stalagmite: a cave formation that sticks up from the floor, often under a stalactite.

steamboat: a boat with a paddle wheel that is turned by a steam engine.

steam engine: an engine that burns wood or coal to heat water and create steam. The steam generates power to run the engine.

subduction: when one tectonic plate slides underneath another tectonic plate.

supercell: a severe thunderstorm with strong updrafts and downdrafts of air. Supercells often have large hail, strong winds, downpours, and sometimes tornadoes.

suspension bridge: a bridge whose road is suspended from two or more cables that pass over towers.

swarm: a large number of insects flying together.

tectonic: relating to the forces that produce movement and changes in the earth's crust.

the Midwest: another name for the Great Plains in the middle of the United States.

thermal: related to heat.

tornado: a violent, twisting, funnel-shaped column of air extending from a thunderstorm to the ground.

transform boundary: where two plates slide against each other.

tributary: a stream or river that flows into a larger river.

U-shaped valley: a valley that has been carved by a glacier and has a shape like the letter "U," with steep sides and a flat floor.

volcano: a vent in the earth's surface through which magma, ash, and gases erupt.

watershed: the land area that drains into a river or stream.

wetland: an area located around lakes and rivers that contains a lot of soil moisture.

wind shear: a change in the direction of wind, especially when wind blows in different directions at different heights.

zone of ablation: the area on a glacier where snow or ice melts or evaporates.

zone of accumulation: the area on a glacier where snow accumulates.

BOOKS

Anderson, Alan, Gwen Diehn, and Terry Krautwurst. *Geology Crafts for Kids: 50 Nifty Projects to Explore the Marvels of Planet Earth*. New York: Sterling, 1998.

Bennett, Clayton. *Montant (Celebrate the States, Second)*. New York: Marshall Cavendish, 2010.

Bennett, Michelle and Joyce Hart. *Missouri (Celebrate the States, Second)*. New York: Marshall Cavendish, 2010.

Bjorkland, Ruth. *Nebraska (Celebrate the States, Second)*. New York: Marshall Cavendish, 2010.

Blobaum, Cindy and Michael Kline. *Geology Rocks!: 50 Hands-On Activities to Explore the Earth*. Vermont: Williamson Publishing Company, 1999.

Chambers, Catherine. *Life in the Grasslands*. New York: Children's Press, 2005.

Collard, Sneed B. III. *The Prairie Builders: Reconstructing America's Lost Grasslands*. Boston: Houghton Mifflin Boston, 2005.

Farndon, John. *How the Earth Works*. New York: Dorling Kindersley Publishers Ltd, 1999.

Geore, Michael. *Glaciers*. Mankato, Minnesota: Creative Education, Inc., 1991.

Ingram, Scott. *Kansas (From Sea to Shining Sea, Second)*. New York: Children's Press, 2009.

Jensen, Niels R. *Ohio (Checkerboard Geography Library: United States)*. Edina, Minnesota: Checkerboard Books, 2009.

Johnson, Elizabeth. *Michigan (From Sea to Shining Sea, Second)*. New York: Children's Press, 2009.

Johnson, Rebecca L. *A Walk in the Prairie*. Minneapolis: Carolrhoda Books, 2001.

Ling, Bettina. *Wisconsin (From Sea to Shining Sea, Second)*. New York: Children's Press, 2008.

Lynch, Wayne. *Prairie Grasslands*. Minnetonka, Minnesota: NorthWord Books for Young Readers, 2006.

McDaniel, Melissa. *North Dakota (Celebrate the States, Second)*. New York: Marshall Cavendish, 2010.

Miller, Amy. *Colorado (From Sea to Shining Sea, Second)*. New York: Children's Press, 2008.

Nadeau, Isaac. *Glaciers*. New York: Powerkids Press, 2006.

Ollhoff, Jim. *Wyoming (The United States)*. Edina, Minnesota: Checkerboard Books, 2009.

Schwabacher, Martin, and Patricia K. Kummer. *Minnesota (Celebrate the States, Second)*. New York: Marshall Cavendish, 2008.

Smith, Richard. *Indiana (Checkerboard Geography Library: United States)*. Edina Minnesota: Checkerboard Books, 2009.

Somervill, Barbara. *Illinois (From Sea to Shining Sea, Second)*. New York: Children's Press, 2008.

Wheeler, Jill C. *Iowa (United States)*. Edina, Minnesota: Abdo Publishing Company, 2009.

Yacowitz, Caryn. *South Dakota (From Sea to Shining Sea, Second)*. New York: Children's Press, 2009.

WEB SITES

- **www.maps.google.com** Satellite view of the Great Plains and Mountain West. Click on the Satellite tab and scroll to wherever you want to look. You can zoom in or out.

- **www.nps.gov/** National Park Service main web site. Click on links to find specific national parks and monuments.

- **http://mineralsciences.si.edu/tdpmap/** World Interactive Map of Volcanoes, Earthquakes, Impact Craters, and Plate Tectonics, by Smithsonian, USGS, and US Naval Research Laboratory.

- **http://earthquake.usgs.gov/earthquakes/** Earthquakes in all states. Click on link on the left called "Earthquake Lists & Maps, then click on link "By State" to view information about a particular state. There are lots of other links with interesting information.

- **http://earthquake.usgs.gov/learn/kids/** U.S. Geological Survey (U.S.G.S.) Earthquakes for Kids site.

- **http://volcanoes.usgs.gov/yvo/activity/monitoring/** Web site of active volcanic monitoring of Yellowstone National Park.

- **www.nps.gov/yell/naturescience/volcanoqa.htm** Yellowstone National Park questions and answers.

- **www.nps.gov/iatr/index.htm** Ice Age National Scenic Trail.

- **www.nssl.noaa.gov/primer/tornado/tor_climatology.html** National Oceanic and Atmospheric Administration, general information about tornadoes.

- **www.usatoday.com/weather/resources/askjack/archives-weather-extremes.htm** Questions and Answers about Weather facts.

- **www.americanrivers.org/about-rivers/** Rivers: facts about rivers, dams, river songs, and more.

- **http://water.usgs.gov/** Water Resources in the U.S. by the USGS.

- **www.tallgrass.org** Friends of the Prairie Learning Center, Neal Smith National Wildlife Refuge.

- **www.42explore.com/prairie.htm** 42eXplore – this site has cool information about all kinds of stuff, including prairies (click on the Main Menu to see other topics).

- **www.nationalgeographic.com/features/98/burrow/** Prairie dogs.

- **http://coseegreatlakes.net/curriculum/** Great Lakes: Projects and information.

- **www.epa.gov/glnpo/image/** Visualizing the Great Lakes: a library of pictures from the Great Lakes.

- **www.glerl.noaa.gov/data/** NOAA Great Lakes Environmental Research Laboratory.

INDEX

Asian Carp

INDEX